Good Takeoffs
and Good Landings

2nd Edition

TAB
PRACTICAL
FLYING SERIES

Good Takeoffs
and Good Landings

2nd Edition

Joe Christy

revised and updated by
Ken George

TAB BOOKS

Blue Ridge Summit, PA

SECOND EDITION
FIRST PRINTING

© 1991 by **TAB Books**.
TAB Books is a division of McGraw-Hill, Inc.

Library of Congress Cataloging-in-Publication Data

Christy, Joe.
    Good takeoffs and good landings / by Joe Christy, revised and updated by Ken George — 2nd ed.
      p.   cm.
    Includes index.
    ISBN 0-8306-7611-2 (hardbound)   ISBN 0-8306-3611-0 (pbk.)
      1. Airplanes—Landing. 2. Airplanes—Takeoff. I. Title.
  II. Title: Good take offs and good landings.
  TL711.L3C48 1991   91-2227
  629.132′5213—dc20   CIP

TAB Books offers software for sale. For information and a catalog, please contact TAB Software Department, Blue Ridge Summit, PA 17294-0850.

Acquisitions Editor: Jeff Worsinger
Book Editor: Tracey L. May
Production: Katherine G. Brown
Series Design: Jaclyn J. Boone
Cover Photograph: Brent Blair, Harrisburg, PA

Contents

To Joe Christy
1918–1988

Introduction

IF THERE IS A SINGLE PREREQUISITE FOR MAKING CONSISTENTLY good takeoffs and landings, it is that you have to work at it—new student pilot or 10,000-hour veteran, you have to work at it. It never gets any easier; it just seems easier to those who develop good techniques and to whom precision becomes a habit.

The problem is, there is no single procedure that is effective in all conditions, and the last thing a student or low-time pilot wants to hear is that "it takes experience." Experience is a tardy teacher.

There are stylized procedures that will ensure safe and acceptable takeoffs and landings under most conditions. These are what you learn by rote—the things you can do by the numbers. Add some common sense, along with a thorough understanding of the aerodynamic forces involved, and you can—with effort and concentration—ad-lib the fine tuning required to make enviable takeoffs and landings.

The "aerodynamic forces involved" are, of course, the true keys, and we will make a detailed investigation of them with regard to control-handling techniques and your assessment of each takeoff and landing situation.

Included are the common transitional operations attendant to takeoffs and landings, as well as radio communications procedures, because all have a bearing—either directly or indirectly—upon the planning and execution of these actions.

This book is intended as a practical, hands-on guide for beginning and low-time pilots. I've avoided theory and mathematical formulas in favor of straightforward, useful data and advice.

The second edition has been expanded to include information about the importance of clean aircraft windows for excellent visibility, anecdotal stories about actual flying experiences, the importance of staying with a disabled aircraft as the pilot in command, and a density altitude review. Updated glossaries include a look at basic procedures for takeoff, go-around, and landing, plus a review of selected National Transportation Safety Board takeoff and landing accidents.

1
The Basics

OVER THE YEARS, MUCH HAS BEEN SAID ABOUT THE "TRUE" functions of an airplane's flight controls. I know an instructor who tells his students that the rudder should be regarded as a "trimming device." My instructor, back in the 1930s, was fond of saying that you should think of the throttle as the "up-and-down" control, and other instructors insist that, in or near a stall, wings must be leveled with rudder, never aileron.

Nothing is wrong with any of the above, although each could stand some elaboration. There are a lot of "howevers" in flying, and it's necessary to qualify just about everything you say about the action and effect of the flight controls. For example many instructors like to say that "pitch plus power equals performance." That, too, is correct, but it doesn't say where the power comes from. With no thrust from the engine, the aircraft glides, using gravity for power—if you have previously stored sufficient energy in the form of altitude.

That touches on one of the secrets of safe flight—*stored energy*. As long as you have excess speed or altitude to spend, you have a margin of safety, and these two forms of energy are almost always interchangeable. That is what makes it possible to teach that there are times when the control wheel controls altitude (an instrument approach, for example), and times when the control wheel controls airspeed (during climbout following takeoff, for example).

Actually, it's all in the way you think about it. During climbout, you are controlling the rate of climb by referencing the airspeed. If you had an angle-of-attack indicator, it would serve the same purpose (if your owner's manual classified climbs that way), because that is what you are actually controlling with the forward and backward movement of the control wheel.

ANGLE OF ATTACK

The whole story of controlled flight is contained in a single term: *angle of attack*. Everything an airplane does in flight depends upon the angle at which its wing meets the supporting sea of air. If air were visible, flying would be easier, because we could see what was happening as the air flowed over and around the wings; but because it is not, we avoid talking about angles of attack as much as possible, and refer instead to the

Fig. 1-1. The three axes of an aircraft are shown in this photograph of a Beech Aircraft Corporation Musketeer. Pitch is controlled by the elevators (stabilator in this case), yaw is controlled by the rudder, and roll (bank) is controlled by the ailerons.

"pitch" attitude of our aircraft (FIG. 1-1); the nose is pitched up and pitched down—despite the fact that "up" and "down" are not always up and down in relation to the direction you want the nose to go. It's better to say that up-elevator (back pressure on the control wheel) pulls the nose toward the pilot, while down-elevator (forward pressure on the control wheel) pushes the nose away from the pilot, or, back pressure increases angle of attack, and forward pressure decreases angle of attack. *These statements are true regardless of an airplane's attitude in relation to the ground.*

Angle of attack is more precisely defined as the angle between the *chord line* of the wing (a straight line from the foremost point of the leading edge to the trailing edge) and the *relative wind.* Relative wind results from the movement of an aircraft through the air; it is the airflow over an airfoil and is parallel to and in the opposite direction of the flight path of the airplane (FIG. 1-2).

Maximum angle of attack is between 15° and 18°, no matter what the airspeed, attitude, or other flight condition. Tip the wing up at an angle greater than this critical angle, and the smooth airflow around the wing—especially over its upper surfaces, which provide most of the lift—is broken up and the wing stalls.

Normally, you have no reason to exceed an angle of attack greater than about 10°. Your best *rate* of climb will be less than that, and although best *angle* of climb can be as much as 15° (and therefore nibbling at the edge of a stall), it is not exactly a normal maneuver. In any

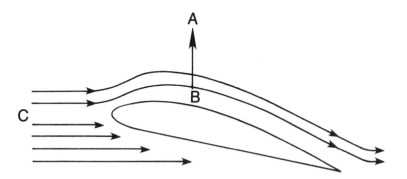

Fig. 1-2. The relative wind results from the movement of an aircraft through the air (C). The low-pressure area (B) is created by the wing's shape. The center of lift (A) moves forward as the angle of attack increases. At extreme angles of attack, the airflow over the wing's upper surface begins to burble at the trailing edge and moves forward, following the center of lift until lift is destroyed, unless angle of attack is reduced.

case, these figures are not very useful in the real world, because no one can accurately eyeball such measurements, especially when the wings are not level. True, the artificial horizon will show a 10° climb, but that indicates where the nose is pointing, not necessarily with respect to the relative wind.

Flying in visual meteorological conditions, pilots judge the safe angle-of-attack range primarily by reference to external indicators—aircraft nose and wingtips in relation to the horizon—backed up by a check of the attitude indicator and perhaps the airspeed indicator. The vertical-speed indicator (VSI) tells us a little something about angle of attack only indirectly and has a significant lag to boot. The attitude indicator (artificial horizon) provides instant information, and you can easily determine a 10° positive angle of attack from it when the wings are fairly level (with a little effort, perhaps, in turning flight). Ten degrees, plus the built-in angle of incidence (which can be as much as 3°), begins to crowd maximum allowable angle of attack.

So, it isn't too hard to visualize the angle of attack in level flight. It's when you start to turn that the angle-of-attack indicators—both outside and in the cockpit—become fuzzy.

You do have other indicators. One of them is G-load. My instructor back in the stone age of flight had a favorite saying: "Keep the load off yourself and you won't overload the airplane."

He as talking about G-load, of course, and his idea of an acceptable G-load ranged between the approximately 1.2 Gs of a 30° banked turn, and the 1.4 Gs of a 45° banked turn. He frowned on turns banked beyond 45° but like to demonstrate them at 60° and tell his students that they, and the airplane, possessed twice their normal weight in such a turn—which was, of course, self-evident (FIG. 1-3).

Fig 1-3. Keep the load off yourself and you will never overload an airplane. Recall that the higher the airspeed when an airplane is stalled, the higher the load factor.

He even had a "strain gauge" for the wings that was a most effective device for convincing students that excessive back pressure on the control stick was to be avoided lest the wings suddenly depart the aircraft. The strain gauge was a length of soft baling wire that ran from the point between the wings of the Spartan biplane where the flying and landing wires crossed to the engine mount. Normally, the wire was loose, and I never was sure whether my instructor actually knew how much of a G-load was required to make the wire tight. He claimed that the wings had to bend backwards four inches to tighten the strain gauge. I'm not sure that I believed that. But if you ever saw that bit of wire vibrating taut as a bow string, I doubt you'd ever forget it. I never have.

Another indication that angle of attack is significantly increasing and airspeed is decreasing, is a loosening-up of the controls, a situation that you should recognize from slow-flight practice during initial instruction. Perhaps your instructor mentioned that slow flight equates with increased angles of attack. You probably noticed that, in slow flight, the nose rode a little higher in relation to the horizon.

The airspeed indicator is an indirect source of angle-of-attack information. In turning flight, it is second only to the attitude indicator for such reference. You can, of course, temporarily exceed the wings' critical angle of attack at *any* airspeed with abrupt and excessive back pressure on the control yoke, but operating in normal flight regimes, applying normal control pressures, you can rely on the airspeed indicator to provide information relative to the stall.

FOUR BASIC FLIGHT CONDITIONS

Any instructor will tell you, the better how-to-fly books will tell you, and I will tell you: You cannot hope to become a truly competent pilot until you have mastered the four basic flight conditions—straight-and-level, climbs, turns, and descents. All flight maneuvers involve one or more of these conditions, including takeoffs and landings. You will not be able to consistently perform good takeoffs and landings until the four fundamentals are consistently flown with a high degree of precision.

It's not easy. The books that say how easy it is to learn to fly were written to sell, not to use. Sure, after 10 or 12 hours of dual almost anyone can take off, smoke around the pattern, and get the airplane back on the ground right side up. To those who decide that is good enough, one of two things will eventually happen: they will kill themselves (and probably several others, as well) in an airplane, or they will luck-out of a situation that frightens them to the edge of panic and then decide to quit flying. Rarely do incompetent pilots decide to expend the effort necessary to become safe and competent pilots. Had they possessed the "right stuff," they would have established a higher goal in the first place.

So, I recommend that you be honest about your goals as a pilot. If you have a track record of not finishing things you start, if you habitually seek the easiest way to do things, and if you regularly spend more money than you earn, the sensible course is to forget flying and instead take of an activity that is less exacting in its demands on you.

STRAIGHT AND LEVEL

Most flight instructors will initiate flight training with straight-and-level practice. Some students are impatient with such a prosaic approach to learning to fly, but that is where precision begins, and the ability to hold a heading within 10° will determine your score on the FAA private

Fig. 1-4. Establishment of inside and outside reference points is essential to the precision of straight and level flying.

flight test (5° on more advanced tests). You'll have to be even more precise during instrument landing approaches.

The ability to hold a constant altitude, with wings level, is the rest of the equation. It takes practice, and the mental practice is as important as the physical practice. You are not only imposing upon your nervous system the countless tiny corrections necessary for good straight-and-level, but you are also impressing the *habit* of precision upon your mind (FIG. 1-4).

The proliferation of affordable autopilots in lightplanes tends to erode pilot proficiency in straight-and-level flight because the autopilot will fly the airplane in cross-country cruise with great precision, while significantly decreasing pilot fatigue. If an airplane is so equipped, periodically give "George" a rest and hand-fly it.

In VFR conditions, straight-and-level indicators are primarily outside the airplane—the position of the engine cowling and wingtips in relation to the horizon—backed up by a quick scan of two or three flight instruments. Actually, a glance at the attitude indicator should be sufficient because it indicates both pitch and bank.

Several flight instruments report changes in attitude. The VSI, the altimeter, and the airspeed indicator will all gain or lose with changes in pitch and no compensating change in power.

If an airplane has no directional gyro, the turn coordinator is hard to beat for detecting heading changes as they occur in this kind of practice. Navigating cross-country, you'll be using the VOR course deviation needle or magnetic compass for directional guidance.

Once stabilized on what you believe to be straight-and-level (transitions to straight-and-level from climbs and descents will be discussed momentarily) with the desired power, mixture, and rpm settings, check the attitude indicator and VSI to confirm zero pitch; then refocus your attention to external references.

Observe where the wingtips ride in relation to the horizon. When viewed from between the two front seats, both left and right tips will be the same distance above (for high-wings) or below (for low-wings) that reference. Note, too, the amount that the leading edges are tipped upward. Then snap a mental picture of how the top of the engine cowling appears in relation to the horizon ahead. In most lightplanes, the top of the cowling, depending upon where along its sloping surface your line of sight is fixed, will be several inches below the horizon. You will quickly establish your own mental images of the external straight-and-level indicators for each airplane you fly.

STYLIZED SCAN

The need to remain vigilant for other air traffic and to learn to divide attention between the outside and inside of an aircraft argues for the development of a scanning habit that provides an ongoing visual check of the sky around you, includes the external straight-and-level references, and instills an "instrument awareness" factor in your mind. It is a simple concept and one that is easy to initiate.

Start anywhere and vary the sequence to suit yourself. The important thing is to develop a stylized scan habit so that you will do it without conscious thought. Begin by looking as far behind the left wing as possible without straining. Then, at a measured pace—not slow, not fast—turn your head to allow your gaze to sweep from left to right outside the airplane, noting the cowl/horizon reference (and a distant landmark if using such to maintain a track by pilotage). Continue the scan as far to the right as you can comfortably see. (Whenever you have a passenger in the right seat, put him or her to work watching for traffic on the right.) On the return sweep, include the instrument panel.

If you are familiar with the airplane it isn't necessary to actually *read* instruments and gauges most of the time. You will know where the needles should be pointing, and any that are out of place will stand out. Scanning frequency is up to you and can be influenced by weather, type and density of traffic, visibility, and the type of airplane.

Your scan can be a very effective safety procedure in the airport traffic pattern. Because your attention must constantly be divided between inside and outside indicators in the pattern, you undoubtedly will abbreviate the scan somewhat, but you must not ignore the instrument panel.

TURNS

Most accidents in airport traffic patterns occur during turns—turns from the downwind to base leg, and from base to final approach (FIG. 1-5). The accidents happen as the result of a stalled condition, usually with crossed controls—in other words, in steep turns. If we stop and consider all the things that are against us in steep turns (more than, say, 35° of bank), most of us would avoid them like the plague: 1. The steeper the turn, the more you give up in the way of external references that aid in maintaining level flight. 2. The airspeed indicator is subject to error. 3. The G-load causes an increase in stall speed. 4. You are led into a crossed-control situation that, after about 40–45° of bank, seems to indicate that nothing is working the way it should.

Fig. 1-5. Every turn in the traffic pattern should be shallow, approximately 10 to 15 degrees of banking, for instance. A go-around is the safer option if a steep turn might be required to correct poor timing and improper judgment.

The airplane has a marked tendency to increase the bank angle, and you must hold opposite aileron against that force. Meanwhile, you feel the need to feed-in more and more rudder (in the direction of the turn) to maintain a constant turn rate, while increasing the back pressure on the control yoke to "pull" the airplane around the turn. With the horizon ahead tilted at 45° or more, it is no longer very useful as a pitch reference.

The stall warner sounds and, if you have time (remember, you are 800 – 1,000 feet agl), your next inclination is to check the airspeed indicator, but that reading doesn't seem to make sense. The relative wind is entering the pitot head at an angle, and perhaps buffeting the static port as well. Without quick and proper action at this point, most airplanes will stall, whip inverted, and dive into the ground. This happens a predictable number of times each year.

Sure, it's depressing, but reduced-speed turns at low altitude are part of every airport traffic pattern. There is no way you can avoid performing them, but you *can* master them.

You know how to make normal turns, banked 30° or less, and as a private pilot you could fly for years without exceeding 35° of bank. The secret is good planning. No matter how much it hurts, you've got to *think* in an airplane.

Practicing turns, you should turn a predetermined about—say 90° to a new heading. Then practice turns of 45°, 180°, and 360°. If you do your 360s properly you might feel the bump of your aircraft propwash as you return to your original heading. You should practice turns referenced to an external landmark and turns referenced to the directional gyro. They are not the same.

Certain pilots believe that the turn coordinator, which has largely replaced the old needle-and-ball instrument, indicates angle of bank. It does not. What it tells you is direction and *rate* of turn. The little airplane merely replaced the gyro-controlled needle of the earlier instrument. Many pilots have been taught to *step on the ball* when it moves from its cage. Actually, you can *cage* the ball two ways: If the ball sinks to the inside of your turn, you can add rudder or reduce bank; if the ball rises to the outside of your turn, you can reduce rudder or add bank.

I maintain that stepping on the ball is inefficient, and in heavy aircraft—that is, heavier than a training airplane—it is dangerous at low airspeeds. Some years ago, the Army taught it one way, the Navy another. A friend who is a pilot instructor in Air Force C-5As says he was taught that ailerons control the ball and rudder controls the needle.

Clearly, it is taught both ways, but I believe one way is more consistent with the entire range of flight maneuvers, and is certainly more consistent with safe operating practices at low airspeeds. If you have been taught to step on the ball to cage it, ask your instructor about this. One thing you can almost always count on from a CFI is a good and sincere response to the student pilot who displays an honest desire to work and learn.

WHERE IS THE WIND?

Another of the basics that sometimes causes confusion has to do with the effects of wind on your airplane in flight—perhaps instead of "wind," the direction of movement of the air mass through which you are flying. You must fully understand your relationship with the wind when airborne. If you do, you aren't likely to be trapped into the ancient *downwind turn* controversy in the pilots' lounge (FIG. 1-6). I have a friend who writes about flying and has been a pilot for more than 25 years. He always adds a touch of power when making a downwind turn in the lower altitudes. It doesn't do any harm, and I long ago gave up trying to convince him that

Fig. 1-6. To an airplane in flight, there is no difference between turning downwind, crosswind, or upwind, except when flying through a wind shear.

there is no difference between downwind, upwind, or crosswind turns in flight. They are all the same to the airplane. You will lose a little airspeed during *any* level turn—not because of any wind effect, but because part of the total energy is diverted to lift the airplane around the turn. Vertical lift no longer offsets gravity when a bank is established, because the wings' lift, the total lift, is at an angle to gravity's pull. Back pressure on the yoke increases angle of attack and compensates for the loss of vertical lift. But without an increase in power, the price paid is a slight drop in airspeed during the turn, regardless of wind direction.

I once heard an experienced agricultural pilot say that he could feel the difference between downwind and upwind turns. Close to the surface, the difference is certainly evident in the ground track, but it is nothing that the airplane can feel. The 90-degree turn from a downwind to a crosswind track requires *more* than a 90-degree heading change. The drift is going to be quite evident close to the ground.

You will turn *less* than 90° to achieve a 90-degree change in ground track when turning from upwind to crosswind. Remember, when airborne, you are carried *with* a moving air mass independently of your movement *through* it. The ground track maneuvers practiced as a student pilot are supposed to give you an understanding of this relationship.

Entering a turn, *coordinate* yoke and rudder. The exact amount of rudder required for a given bank angle is a thing you learn by doing. In medium-banked turns in most lightplanes, you will return the controls to neutral after the turn is established. In shallow turns, you will have to hold some control pressures into the turn because the dihedral (the angle at which the wings are joined to the fuselage) tends to return the aircraft to level flight. In steep turns, you will find yourself holding opposite aileron to counter the airplane's overbanking tendency after you exceed about 45° of bank. No single set of instructions covers control techniques in all kinds of turns.

You will lead your recovery from a turn by an amount commensurate with the turn rate. I wish I could think of a way to say that more precisely, but again, this is one of the things you have to learn by doing. The feel of the airplane controls, like the feel of your automobile's controls, is memorized by your nervous system and soon becomes automatic. In controlling an airplane, however, you have to consider a third dimension, and you can't trust your nervous system when it is denied input from your eyes.

When you bank the airplane, the down aileron adds both lift and drag on its side. That wing rises, but also momentarily slows, which causes the nose to yaw towards the up wing. That is why, to make a balanced turn, you need to feed-in rudder in the direction of the turn. Too much rudder and you'll *skid* the turn, while too little rudder will allow the airplane to *slip* toward the inside of the turn.

Another force is involved here—that of the propeller. I will get to it momentarily because it is to be reckoned with in takeoff and climb as well.

Earlier, I mentioned *stored energy* and the fact that altitude, range, and airspeed are on deposit in the same account. To a limited extent, all are interchangeable; spend one and you are left with more of the others.

While discussing this subject in another book, I suggested a simple demonstration that I picked up from an instructor friend: You are trimmed for straight-and-level flight, cruising at 65-percent power. Now, without moving any other controls, advance the throttle. Do you speed up? No. You begin to climb.

You were straight-and-level, and you didn't pull back the wheel to raise the nose. Why didn't you simply gain airspeed?

Well, additional power meant more lift at that angle of attack. Had you wanted to increase airspeed, it would have been necessary to decrease your angle of attack when you added more power. You see, when you were straight-and-level, using 65-percent of your available power, you had the airplane trimmed to whatever angle of attack was required to exactly balance lift against gravity. Additional power meant added lift. You could have remained straight-and-level and increased airspeed by applying forward pressure on the control wheel and then retrimming to fly at the decreased angle of attack.

Fig. 1-7. Back pressure on the yoke in cruising flight produces a momentary climb at the expense of airspeed. Recall that the primary climb control is the throttle for additional engine power to perform the climb.

You could have climbed by applying back pressure on the control wheel, for awhile, at least, in which case you would have done so at the expense of airspeed (FIG. 1-7). Such a trade-off is limited because it requires that you have excess airspeed (thrust) to be traded. Back pressure on the control wheel increases the angle of attack, and that demands additional thrust—thrust that must be subtracted from the straight-and-level thrust.

In practice, you will normally make minor altitude corrections with pitch—with back pressure or forward pressure on the control wheel—because the airspeed changes are relatively insignificant. And learning to fly instruments, you will be told to control altitude with pitch and airspeed with power. On instruments, power and pitch adjustments are small, however, and your throttle remains the primary up-and-down control. As I said, there are a lot of *howevers* in flying.

TORQUE AND P-FACTOR

In the process of converting the engine's power into usable thrust, the propeller creates *torque*, and when the airplane is in any attitude except straight-and-level, the propeller is also responsible for a force known as *P-factor*.

Propeller torque is an example of Newton's Third Law of Motion, which holds that for every action there is an equal and opposite reaction. The crankshafts and the propellers of aircraft piston engines manufactured in the United States rotate clockwise as viewed by the pilot, assuming that the engine is on the front of the airplane. The equal and opposite reaction to the propeller's clockwise rotation is a twisting force in the opposite direction (counterclockwise) exerted on the engine and airframe.

Because the airplane's mass far exceeds that of the propeller, this part of the propeller's side effects is relatively insignificant in lightplanes. It is, however, reinforced by the effect of *spiraling propwash*. *Propwash* is an ancient term that describes the disturbed air sent back by the propeller. As air is dragged through the rotating propeller blades, it is thrust rearward in a spiraling motion. This twisting column of air strikes the *left* side of the fuselage and vertical stabilizer to produce a yawing force to the left.

The combined effects of propeller torque and spiraling propwash require some right rudder for correction at airspeeds below normal cruise. The airplane is rigged, usually with an offset vertical stabilizer or engine mounting, to compensate for propeller torque at normal cruising airspeeds.

P-factor, which becomes evident at low airspeeds with high rpm and high angles of attack, as in a climb, is owed to the fact that the descending propeller blade (on the right side as viewed by the pilot) meets the oncoming air at a greater angle of attack than the ascending blade. More thrust is generated on the right side in the nose-up attitude. This, too, contributes to a left-turning tendency, and is yet another reason that right rudder is needed during takeoff and climb.

CLIMBS

VFR climbs should be performed using flight instruments and outside visual references. Shallow *S-turns* during climb help clear forward blind spots and also make you more visible to other air traffic.

Any kind of climbing turn takes practice because, if you are to maintain a constant turn rate and bank angle, you must have good coordination in pitch, roll, and yaw simultaneously. You cannot expect to hold a constant airspeed and pitch attitude because you must pay for the turn with lift and airspeed.

Straight climbs are fairly simple in training airplanes. You usually climb at full throttle, adjust airspeed with pitch to hold V_y (best climb rate) or slightly faster as instructed by the owner's manual, and trim away control-wheel back pressure. Due to torque effect and P-factor, slight right rudder is necessary to counter the left-turning tendency. Because the nose of the airplane obscures the ground directly ahead, you reference the directional gyro to maintain a straight track. The wingtips can be useful to maintain a straight track if there is a highway, railroad, or some other prominent surface feature some distance away and parallel to your track.

In high-performance lightplanes, you have additional considerations. If the engine has a takeoff power rating and a maximum continuous rating, you must reduce power shortly after takeoff. Most pilots reduce power after takeoff even when there is no requirement to do so. With most engines, there's no reason why you can't climb at full power as long as the engine gauges remain in their green ranges.

Equipped with a constant-speed propeller, when reducing power after takeoff, back off the throttle (manifold pressure) first and then the propeller control (rpm), except on geared Lycomings. Normally aspirated engines will lose about 1 ″ Hg per 1,000 feet of altitude during climb.

Some lightplane pilots, flying the simpler machines, do not adjust the mixture control until leveling off for cruising flight, especially if climbing at full throttle, under the assumption that the rich mixture is helping to cool the cylinder heads and exhaust valves. If you select a prolonged cruise-climb to get across country faster, you might want to lean the mixture to about 150 °F on the rich side of peak EGT, and remember that the cowl flaps are the primary means of regulating *cylinder head temperature* (CHT), which should not exceed 450 °F.

The time-honored procedure with the smaller engines, equipped with fixed-pitch props is to lean until the engine begins to run a little rough and then enrichen the mixture enough to smooth it out. Monitor the oil temperature if it is the only engine heat gauge and further enrich the mixture as necessary. The main reason that air-cooled engines get poorer fuel economy than liquid-cooled engines is that air-cooled engines require richer fuel mixtures to hold down cylinder-head and exhaust-valve/valve-guide temperatures.

Anticipate leveling off before reaching the desired altitude. Start to level off approximately 50 feet below selected cruise altitude. Lower the nose gradually, and retrim the airplane. You will lose altitude if you lower the nose to level flight without allowing the airspeed to build proportionately.

To accelerate to the desired cruising speed, temporarily maintain climb power after the airplane is in a level attitude. When you reach the desired cruising airspeed, or slightly faster, back off the throttle to the selected cruise power, adjust the mixture control, and retrim. If your aircraft is equipped with a constant-speed propeller, when reducing power always retard the throttle first, then the rpm; when increasing power, always adjust the rpm first, then advance the throttle.

There is no precise correlation between manifold pressure and rpm. Any combination is acceptable as long as it produces the desired result and the associated engine gauges behave. During World War II, Charles Lindbergh went to the Pacific to show P-38 pilots how to greatly increase the range of their aircraft with high manifold pressure and low rpm settings.

GLIDES AND DESCENTS

You can intentionally descend with partial power or no power. With power off you adjust the pitch attitude to maintain airspeed and accept whatever rate of descent results. With partial power, use the amount of power needed to obtain the desired airspeed, while controlling the rate of descent with pitch attitude.

To initiate a power-off descent, first apply carburetor heat about one minute before starting the descent, and then back off the throttle. Never *chop* the throttle; there is no normal situation in which the throttle should be operated abruptly.

Reduced torque will require some corrective left rudder. Hold the nose level until the airspeed drops to near the normal descent airspeed, then lower the nose and establish the proper airspeed with the control wheel. Trim away the control-wheel pressure. The descent airspeed with power off is usually about 1.3 times the stall speed and close to the airplane's best rate-of-climb airspeed.

When the descent is stabilized, make shallow S-turns in order to clear the blind spot below your airplane's nose and reduce the possibility of letting down into other traffic. The habit of making clearing or S-turns during climbs and descents is about as prevalent as thorough preflight inspections, and the worst offenders are the guys with fat logbooks and macho images of themselves. Their unspoken message to other pilots, especially to student pilots, is: "Hey, boy, I've been flying so long that the rules don't apply to me. All that safety jazz is for the inexperienced."

Be advised that thorough preflights *are* for everyone. I recall the takeoff crash of an airplane that was not preflighted. A pencil was found jammed in the elevator hinge. Fuel exhaustion (due to a variety of causes, from mud daubers in fuel tank vents to faulty gauges) is a common danger that is sometimes averted by the preflight inspection.

So much for the lecture, now back to descents. A partial-power descent is entered the same as a power-off descent. As you slow to the desired airspeed, lower the nose to the pitch attitude that produces the desired rate of descent as revealed by the VSI, adjust power to maintain the desired airspeed, and then trim away the elevator pressure.

Both types of let-downs are terminated the same way. Lead the recovery as you do when leveling off from a climb, otherwise, inertia will carry the aircraft below the intended altitude. Smoothly add power as you raise the nose to a level attitude, and then retrim. Return the carburetor-heat knob to the *cold* position.

SHOCK COOLING

Not long ago, a highly experienced aircraft mechanic told me he'd wager that at least half of all the engines in civilian training planes have cracked cylinder heads. When I asked him what prompted such a statement, he explained that trainers, such as the Cessna 150/152, are more subject to shock cooling than other lightplanes. He added the unsettling statement that too many young flight instructors today are careless about teaching students proper engine operating procedures, and this lack of knowledge is carried over into the student's future flying in larger aircraft, resulting in expensive damage to those engines.

Monitoring engine gauges and keeping those needles corralled in safe operating ranges is not enough. Rough handling of the throttle can damage an engine, as can *shock cooling*. Shock cooling to an air-cooled airplane engine occurs when the engine is allowed (or forced) to cool too rapidly, usually during letdown following extended cruise. All parts of an operating engine are not the same temperature. The cylinder heads, exhaust valves, and valve guides function at much higher temperatures than the rest of the engine and are the components most at risk if the engine cools too quickly.

The hairline cracks that can result from shock cooling of the cylinder heads are most common around the exhaust valve seats and radiating from spark plug holes. The valves can stick and warp, and the exhaust valve seats can become deformed. One common result is bent push rods caused by sticking valves. All of this argues in favor of partial-power descents to prevent shock cooling.

The need to develop a smooth, unhurried touch on the throttle will be magnified anytime you are flying an engine that has counterweights on the crankshaft. This includes most medium- and higher-horsepower lightplane engines. The counterweights have a pendulum action and must adjust to rpm changes; if you chop the throttle on one of these engines, the counterweight bushings can be ruined. Damaged counterweight bushings can lead to broken crankshafts, which can lead to the poorhouse at today's engine overhaul costs.

STUDENT ATTITUDE

Your attitude toward the learning process is extremely important as a student pilot—and for the rest of your flying career, for that matter. There is no such thing as a "born pilot," except those that hatch from eggs. Good pilots don't just happen, they develop, properly directed, through the application of serious effort. That effort is sustained by a strong desire (need?) to excel, along with whatever other factors there might be that mark the high achiever. Your instructor can't give it to you. You bring it with you to the airport if you have it.

If you are a male, I hope that you will resist any tendency to assume the role of the strong, silent type. This usually masks a fear of making an embarrassing mistake or asking a silly question. And this is why some instructors will tell you that women often make better flight students than men. Most women aren't afraid to ask a silly question; and when they blow a maneuver they merely shrug it off and try again. They are not embarrassed by learning errors. No one should be.

In ground school, a lot of student pilots are secretly grateful for the one who has the courage to ask the "silly" questions. They, too, need the answers but don't ask because they don't want to reveal their ignorance. We are all ignorant of subjects new to us. There should be no embarrassment in that.

BETTER VISIBILITY

What is perhaps the most important fuselage component is often overlooked as a safety feature: Plexiglas. Pioneer pilots of open cockpit aircraft had very little to worry about, merely wiping foreign matter from their goggles and focusing through any goggle scratches; presumably any wind screen in front of the cockpit would be cleaned as necessary during flight or upon landing. Plexiglas surrounding closed cockpit aircraft definitely made flying more comfortable inside the aircraft but did not eliminate cleaning.

Clear viewing is the backbone of scanning outside the cockpit to see air traffic, obstructions, or airport features. The fact that all three elements come into play during takeoff and landing makes a clean windshield and clean windows extremely important.

Clean windows might be the most apparent attribute of a new aircraft. Countless hours of research and development over the years permit modern manufacturers to produce a distortion-free window for comfort and safety. Unfortunately, that fresh piece of Plexiglas is often the most abused part of the new aircraft and starts to lose its new lustre almost immediately; beyond natural exposure to the elements, along comes a well meaning line attendant who uses yesterday's rag for today's windshield cleaning, perhaps with a cleaning material that is not recommended for Plexiglas. Conscientious pilots might want to place a sign on the dashboard to discourage unwanted cleaning by inexperienced personnel; the sign would never be a guaranteed stopper, merely a deterrent.

Aircraft owners and conscientious renters who want to preserve or improve the quality of the aircraft Plexiglas should investigate and determine a proper course of action. Consider asking the owner of an older aircraft with spotless windows how he maintains the like-new clarity of the glass in his 15-, 20-, or 25-year-old aircraft. A well-stocked FBO should carry suitable cleaners and waxes, as should a pilot supply store. Popular aviation mail order catalogs have a good selection of products.

When cleaning and polishing aircraft windows, the idea is not to merely clean and polish but to maintain the clarity and finish; maintenance is the key. One pilot's solution seemed like a successful plan: Clean the windows at the conclusion of each flight. In the baggage area of his plane this pilot stored a small plastic bucket and sponge. At the end of each flight, he simply filled the bucket with warm water, immersed the sponge in the water, and applied water to the windshield to soak bugs and other foreign matter from it. Soaking proved beneficial because the formerly dried and caked matter would easily wipe away with the sponge, without bearing down with elbow-grease that could scratch the windows. Plexiglas cleaner and polish would normally be applied in the home hangar, or periodically during a lengthy trip. The same aircraft owner kept a bucket of water in the hangar to similarly soak and wipe down the leading edges to remove bugs and foreign matter and maintain clean airfoils.

DENSITY ALTITUDE

Too often pilots tend to forget the simple fact that high density altitude reduces aircraft performance. Probably the most critical time that density altitude becomes a major factor is upon takeoff, when the aircraft must have 100-percent power to successfully fly and properly climb to clear all obstacles and reach a safe cruising altitude.

Recall that density altitude is pressure altitude (set the altimeter of the aircraft to 29.92 inches of mercury to read the pressure altitude on the dial) corrected for air temperature (read the temperature on the outside air temperature gauge). Density altitude will be higher than pressure altitude on warm days, when the temperature is above the standard 50 °F. Conversely, density altitude will be lower than pressure altitude on cool days, when the temperature is below the 50 °F standard.

Charts and formulas have been around for decades to help pilots determine density altitude; control towers have been known to caution pilots about the likelihood of high density altitude; aviation pocket calculators can solve a density altitude equation more precisely than the popular charts. Determining density altitude is not slave labor, yet too many pilots consider the computation a chore and either inadvertently or purposefully do not take into account applicable conditions.

Effects of high density altitude, which is decreased air density, are noticed during takeoff, while climbing, and when landing. A general rule, according to the FAA, is that a 1,000-foot takeoff run at sea level would double to an approximately 2,000-foot takeoff run at an airport that is 5,000 feet above sea level.

The aircraft wings are supposed to generate enough lift during the takeoff run, which is supposed to reach sufficient velocity to generate the necessary lift. Thin air means more speed is necessary to create enough lift for takeoff, requiring a longer ground run.

Beyond lift for the wings, the engine does not run efficiently because less air is available for combustion in a normally aspirated engine, disregarding turbocharged engines. Again, because the air is thinner, the propeller efficiency is reduced. Obstruction clearance will be critical because the rate of climb is also slower at a high density altitude elevation. Takeoff from a high-altitude airport, commonly in a mountainous area, with rising terrain in the area, on a hot day, requires a density altitude computation—perhaps the takeoff can be scheduled at dawn when the air is cool and more dense than late afternoon. Landing during a period of high density altitude requires a longer landing roll.

2
The Traffic Pattern

MANY AIRPLANES ARE DESTROYED IN AIRPORT TRAFFIC PATTERNS. A few of these are lost to midair collisions, but most stall in steep turns and plunge to the ground with the pilots holding full up-elevator. Ed, a flight instructor I know, says that these crashes occur because traffic patterns are close to the ground. At first, I thought he was joking. He was having a postflight discussion with one of his students, a pleasant young man by the name of Don, and I was an interested bystander.

"You don't believe me?" Ed asked. "Then how come, in good weather, pilots only stall and spin in turns close to the ground? They don't do it higher up."

Don, a senior from the local university, was wary. "If you stall at traffic pattern height," he replied carefully, "there probably isn't enough room to recover." He squinted thoughtfully and added, "Also, you're flying at a lower airspeed in the pattern."

My instructor friend nodded in agreement. "You've correctly identified two factors that contribute to the high fatality rate in the pattern. But what, specifically, makes some traffic pattern turns so dangerous? What are those pilots doing with the controls that they would not do at altitude?"

"Well," Don replied tentatively, "the only thing I can think of is that they might hurry a turn and mess it up."

Ed's smile was wide and beautiful, "Exactly! They are making a turn in relation to a fixed reference on the surface, the runway, and when they discover that they have waited too long to initiate the turn, they try to rack the airplane around in a steep turn." (FIG. 2-1.)

"And that requires a lot of back pressure on the control wheel," Don added, "too much for that airspeed."

"That's most of it," Ed said, obviously proud of his student. "But also consider the position of the other flight controls. The pilot is holding

Fig. 2-1. Misjudging the turn from base leg to final approach might encourage an unwise decision to turn too steep. The steep turn could cause an approach-to-landing stall, helped by the effects of an accelerated stall. This is one attempt to salvage the turn in a right-hand pattern.

a lot of rudder in the direction of the turn attempting to hurry the turn rate, while holding opposite aileron to counter the airplane's overbanking tendency. He is therefore set up for a particularly violent stall. Usually, the airplane will whip inverted and dive into the ground."

I left them at that point, thinking that Ed's original statement about traffic patterns being close to the ground really had little to do with the discussion. Then it occurred to me that Ed had used it as an attention-getter. Frankly, I had always regarded Ed as being a mite on the windy side, but now I took another look at him. He had shared a carefully reasoned explanation with his student and caused his student to think, which is the mark of a good teacher. Ed is also one of those flight instructors who recommend spin training to students.

SPINS

Spins are a part of United States military flight training programs and always have been, and spin training was taken for granted by all civilian instructors for many years. Back in the 1930s, student pilots were required to demonstrate spin recovery before they were allowed to solo. The laws of physics do not change, so why is spin training no longer required in civilian flight training programs?

There are two different theories on this subject. One holds that spin training is unnecessary because you will never allow a stall to progress into a spin if you are properly instructed in stall recovery techniques. Also, because the killer stalls are mostly those entered close to the ground, especially in airport traffic patterns, stall prevention is more important than spin recovery.

The other theory is that spins scared away too many students and potential students.

I believe that you should know how to recover from any unusual flight condition, including an inadvertent spin. If you have not experienced the entire sequence of events in each kind of stall (and its aftermath), you'll never know the full consequences of stalls and how to react to them. This, in turn, can lead to apprehension and doubt at a most inconvenient time.

Personally, I've never understood why the FAA changed its position with regard to spin training. The training wasn't dangerous. Back in the 1920s, before sophisticated instruments and instrument flying procedures were developed, airmail pilots caught above an overcast with fuel running low deliberately spun their big DH-4 biplanes down through the soup and hoped for enough ceiling to allow recovery in clear air. A spin was a known condition, with a relatively slow rate of descent, and it imposed no unusual stresses on the airframe. The wings on one side of the airplane were stalled, and the machine was in a stabilized descent.

In a typical civilian pilot training program, you will encounter only gentle stalls. With power at idle and the wheel all the way back, the average two-place trainer will mush along, bobbing its nose trying to find a flyable angle of attack, and although the VSI will confirm that the airplane is losing altitude, you can rock the wings by turning the control wheel—which is proof enough that you aren't fully stalled. Some instructors will allow you to use the ailerons to pick up a wing if it drops in this situation. You can get by with this for years in a lightly loaded trainer, but it is a dangerous habit to take into airplanes with higher wing loadings. If a wing tends to drop in a stall, pick it up with opposite rudder.

PATTERN PRACTICES

You have a lot of latitude in planning the size and shape of the pattern you fly during a landing approach, even at controlled airports (FIG. 2-2). The FARs do not describe a landing pattern beyond mentioning that any turns are to be made to the left, unless, due to safety or noise abatement considerations, a right-hand pattern is indicated. The FAA does describe recommended traffic pattern procedures in the *Airman's Information Manual* (AIM).

Pattern altitude can extend from 600 to 1,500 feet above ground level (agl), but 1,000 feet is recommended unless "established otherwise." The altitudes apply to propeller-driven lightplanes; jets will fly a higher pattern.

Enter the pattern in level flight at cruising airspeed approximately midway along the downwind leg (earlier in higher-speed aircraft). Enter at a 45-degree angle in order to best observe other traffic. If you must turn away from the pattern to keep from crowding another airplane, make a 360-degree turn away from the pattern. Do the same if you are in the pattern, have the right-of-way, and someone else comes crowding in. He probably doesn't see you.

Once in a while you will encounter a dimwit who will cut you off in the pattern at an uncontrolled field. When you do, the same drill applies; give him room, and remind yourself that it's better to have the idiots in front where you can see them rather than behind where you can't. Remember, whenever you decide to do a 360, advise the tower in advance, or at an uncontrolled field, announce your intentions on the common traffic advisory frequency (CTAF).

Keep in mind while making *any* turn near an airport that you have a big blind spot either above or below the airplane, depending upon where the wing is located (FIG. 2-3).

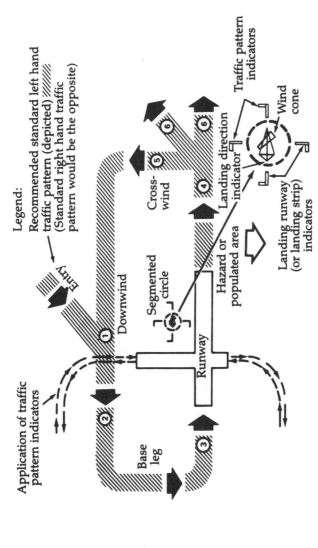

Legend:

Recommended standard left hand traffic pattern (depicted) ///// (Standard right hand traffic pattern would be the opposite)

Application of traffic pattern indicators

Entry

Downwind

Base leg

Segmented circle

Runway

Hazard or populated area

Cross-wind

Landing direction indicator

Landing runway (or landing strip) indicators

Traffic pattern indicators

Wind cone

1. Enter pattern in level flight, abeam the midpoint of the runway, at pattern altitude. (1000' AGL is recommended pattern altitude unless established otherwise.)

2. Maintain pattern altitude until abeam approach end of the landing runway, on downwind leg.

3. Complete turn to final at least ¹⁄₄ mile from the runway.

4. Continue straight ahead until beyond departure end of runway.

5. If remaining in the traffic pattern, commence turn to crosswind leg beyond the departure end of the runway, within 300 feet of pattern altitude.

6. If departing the traffic pattern, continue straight out, or exit with a 45° left turn beyond the departure end of the runway, after reaching pattern altitude.

Fig. 2-2. The FAA's explanation of airport traffic pattern operations.

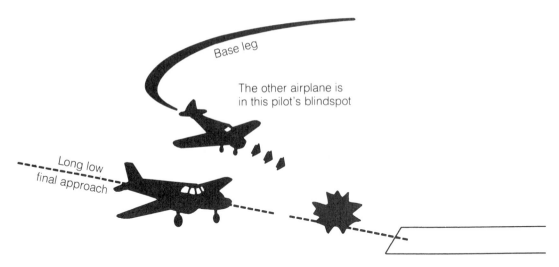

Base leg

The other airplane is
in this pilot's blindspot

Long low
final approach

Fig. 2-3. Midair collisions at uncontrolled airports happen too often when pilots modify the traffic pattern to suit their immediate needs.

Fig. 2-4. Flying the downwind leg at, or slightly less than, the normal cruise airspeed is a great time to get a feel for the aircraft, the airport, and the traffic flow in the air and on the ground.

Maintain the pattern altitude on the downwind leg (FIG. 2-4) until you are abeam of the approach end of the landing runway. Continue on the downwind leg as appropriate to the conditions, normally between $1/4$ and $3/4$ of a mile. Wind velocity and other traffic are the principal factors that will determine the length of a downwind leg. Traffic permitting, many pilots begin the turn to the base leg (FIG. 2-5) when the runway threshold is about 45° behind.

Plan the turn to the final approach so that when you complete the turn you will be properly aligned with the runway, and at least $1/4$ mile from the threshold (FIGS. 2-6 through 2-9). If you are landing at an airport that has parallel runways, make sure that you do not overshoot the turn to final and intrude into the approach airspace of the parallel runway.

On takeoff, if you are departing the pattern, continue straight ahead or exit with a 45-degree left turn (right turn if a right-hand pattern) beyond the departure end of the runway after reaching pattern altitude.

If you are remaining in the pattern, begin the turn to the crosswind leg beyond the departure end of the runway and within 300 feet of pattern altitude.

Fig. 2-5. Another trainer might be on downwind while we are flying the base leg to a touch-and-go landing, which we announced on the CTAF. Perhaps the trainer is not in the traffic pattern because the pilot has not made a position report on the CTAF. A glance over the left shoulder prior to turning for final approach should help ensure that the trainer is not cutting a corner onto a short final approach.

Fig. 2-6. Final approach to the Altus, Oklahoma, Municipal Airport looks good, with no traffic landing or taking off. Two airplanes are seen on the taxiway, but one is still rolling to the end of the taxiway and the other remains in the pre-takeoff, run-up area.

Fig. 2-7. Touchdown on the main landing gear will occur just beyond the runway numbers.

Fig. 2-8. This was at least a smooth landing, if not the best alignment because the aircraft is rolling out to the right of the centerline.

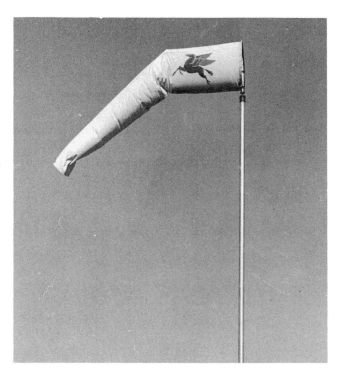

Fig 2-9. A new wind sock is easy to spot from the air. Faded, torn, and tattered socks are occasionally hard to spot, and due to deterioration, the wind might appear more tranquil than it actually is because the sock might not be fully extended.

Plan the pattern and allow for some flexibility to compensate for varying wind and traffic conditions. This flexibility is gained by flying a tighter or looser pattern. If, for example, you are landing into a strong wind, the turn to the base leg will be made sooner than usual and the final approach will be shorter. Wind, visibility, traffic, terrain, and even a housing development below can modify that turn to the base leg.

TOWER-CONTROLLED AIRPORTS

If you are a beginning pilot flying from an airport with an operating control tower, you might have despaired of ever understanding a word of the metallic directives emanating from the overhead radio speaker in the airplane. Not only are the controllers' words unintelligible, but you might be one of those who regard radio communication with much apprehension. If this is the case, the best suggestion is, relax. Transmitting on the radio is one of those relatively simple things that can seem difficult when you try too hard.

You will find it easier to relax if you know what you are doing. The controllers' transmissions become much easier to understand with awareness of the standardized sequence he or she is required to use. Proper use of the radio is an integral part of landing and takeoff operations, including operations from uncontrolled airports.

VISUAL AIRPORT INDICATORS

At many airports, primarily those that are uncontrolled or controlled part-time, you will find a segmented circle near the runway with a wind indicator in its center and traffic pattern direction indicators outside the circle. The wind direction indicator might be the time-honored wind sock (FIG. 2-9) or a wind tee. The tee's cross-bar end points into the wind, as does the fat part of the wind sock. Sometimes, if the wind tee has a wind sock mounted on it or nearby, the tee is manually anchored to indicate the runway in use.

Anytime you have a wind sock for reference, use it. It is the best and most reliable wind direction indicator. It also provides a clue about wind velocity. Occasionally, you will see a tetrahedron, which resembles the delta-shaped paper airplanes you used to sail in study hall. The pointy end of the tetrahedron points in the landing direction, aligned with the active runway. It is not a wind indicator.

Outside the segmented circle you might find traffic pattern indicators, sometimes omitted at airports with the standard left-hand pattern.

Pattern direction indicators will always be displayed if a right-hand pattern is in use, even when no segmented circle is evident.

THE LOW LEVEL WIND SHEAR ALERT SYSTEM (LLWAS)

At certain controlled airports, the tower controller will provide wind shear alerts to arriving and departing aircraft when appropriate. These airports are identified in the *Airport/Facility Directory*. A system of sensors around the airport boundary electronically compares wind data with a sensor near the airport's center to indicate conditions that might result in significant wind shears.

INTERSECTION TAKEOFFS

Intersection takeoffs might be approved, and even initiated, by controllers in order to speed up traffic flow at busy airports.

Controllers are supposed to separate aircraft of 12,500 pounds or less that are taking off from an intersection behind a large or heavy aircraft on the same runway by ensuring at least a three-minute interval between the time the large or heavy airplane takes off and the small airplane begins its takeoff. The controller will usually tell you that you are being held for wake turbulence. If you're the adventurous type, you can tell the controller that you want to waive the three-minute interval, and if the other aircraft isn't heavy, the controller might clear you because you have accepted responsibility for the possible crash.

The three-minute interval rule does not apply when the intersection is 500 feet or less from the runway threshold and a small plane is taking off behind a large plane. The interval is mandatory behind heavy aircraft in all cases.

LIGHTS

At night, or in low visibility situations, strobes or rotating anticollision lights on the airplane should be turned on anytime the engine is operating on the ground, but this is a judgment call. You are encouraged to turn on landing lights when flying within 10 miles of an airport, day or night, in conditions of reduced visibility. Be sure to check the manufacturer's recommendations for the operation of landing lights.

You are aware, of course, that navigation lights must be turned on anytime the engine is operating between sunset and sunrise, but you'd be wise to *always* have them on.

COLLISION AVOIDANCE

The safe separation of air traffic is the primary purpose of ATC. Almost all mid-airs and near misses occur in the vicinity of an airport. There is sufficient possibility of mid-air collisions to make the subject one of concern, although the news media have greatly overstated it. Actually, the FAA said there were 141 "near misses" in 1986 in which two airplanes appeared to come within 100 feet of one another in flight. This was stretched into a total of 828 by including those occasions considered "dangerously close" (up to five miles—five miles being the separation the controllers attempt to maintain between airplanes).

Controllers and electronic wizardry notwithstanding, the final responsibility for in-flight collision avoidance rests with the pilots, and the practical protection you can give to yourself and those "near" to you in the air includes:

1. Be alert to the truly dangerous situations, such as a long final approach that could allow you to let down on top of an airplane hidden from view by the nose of the airplane. Also keep in mind as you turn onto final from base leg that another airplane on an extended final approach might be blocked from view. At uncontrolled fields, another pilot might try to enter the pattern on a short base leg, and he, too, would be blocked from view as you turn from downwind to base leg. The turn from base leg to final approach is probably the most dangerous turn in all of flying because the attention of most pilots is directed at the runway in order to achieve good alignment for the final approach. Here is where it is easy to stall the airplane with crossed controls while hurrying the turn rate, and here is where we tend to be the least observant of other traffic. So the first rule is *vigilance*, and that includes scanning, both inside and outside. Take in as much of the sky as you can, along with frequent checks of the airspeed indicator, turn coordinator, and attitude indicator.

2. The second rule has to be compliance with the rules and standard procedures. The primary purpose of a traffic pattern is the order, or the basis for order, that it imposes on airport traffic. Honor it, and do what everyone else has the right to expect that you will do. It's not enough that you avoid other traffic because you must be avoided as well.

Certain pilots are uncertain about how or where to enter traffic patterns at uncontrolled fields when approaching from any direction except directly into the downwind leg. First, plan a minimal amount of maneuvering above or outside the pattern. For example, if your cross-country course terminates on the non-pattern side of the airport, maintain at least 1,500 feet altitude agl and fly across the airport above pattern altitude.

Continue above and across the pattern, beyond the normal track of the downwind leg, then let down to pattern altitude and turn to the right in a left-hand pattern, to the left in a right-hand pattern, normally about 225°, to enter the downwind leg at the usual 45-degree angle.

Merely enter the upwind leg and fly the crosswind and entire downwind, if you choose. The reason for overflying a strange airport is to find the wind indicator and make sure of the runway in use before entering the pattern.

If the approach to the destination airport is toward the crosswind leg (upwind of the active), it's best to make a shallow turn before reaching the pattern altitude to enter the downwind leg, making sure that you are not crowding anyone who might be in the pattern on upwind or crosswind making touch-and-gos.

The only thing wrong with a long straight-in track to the downwind leg is that it falls into the category of the unexpected. If you choose to enter the pattern that way, be especially alert for aircraft that might enter downwind ahead of you, and always announce your intentions on the CTAF.

It is always best to plan the pattern to allow shallow turns and to never enter a pattern upwind of the departure end of the runway. An airplane that has just become airborne below your altitude can be very hard to see. Preliminary planning for a proper entry to a traffic pattern at a strange uncontrolled airport should be made prior to takeoff with a check of the *Airport/Facility Directory*.

Try not to allow the transgressions of others to influence procedures. There will always be a minority of selfish, self-centered people in all human endeavors, including flying. Occasionally, you will be cut off in the pattern, and you will have to give way to some character with an inventive nature. I once saw a pilot fly the base leg in an opposite direction (that's how he entered the pattern), and then do a tight 270-degree turn onto a short final. He was flying—if that's the word for it—a Temco Swift, and he needed every inch of the 4,500-foot runway. He was dressed like the Red Baron, and clearly was just as dangerous. He was also almost completely out of fuel.

SPACING AND WAKE TURBULENCE

A control tower will take care of the spacing between aircraft, which is the controllers' primary job. But that does not relieve you of the responsibility of avoiding other aircraft as well as their wake turbulence. You will often be reminded of that.

It's unlikely that you will encounter wake turbulence from a heavy aircraft at an uncontrolled airport, but this invisible danger is spawned by all fixed-wing airplanes, its severity being a matter of degree. I had not planned to say much about wake turbulence here because I believed that, surely, everyone had the word on it by this time. I personally haven't heard of a lightplane pilot falling victim to it since a factory test Cessna Skymaster crashed in the wake turbulence of an Air Force jet fighter at Wichita, but in the light of recent developments, perhaps I should try to clearly define this insidious danger.

The main source of the turbulence formed in the wake of fixed-wing airplanes in flight has its genesis in the pressure differential between the air flowing over the top of the wing and that flowing under the bottom of the wing. The pressure beneath is much greater, and this results in the air beneath the wing spilling over the wingtips toward the lower pressure, while the forward motion of the aircraft causes it to roll up in the airflow behind the wing. The ultimate result is a pair of counter-rotating cylindrical vortices, one streaming back from each wingtip, which resemble miniature horizontal tornadoes (FIG. 2-10).

The strength of these vortices depends upon the shape of the wing and the weight and speed of the aircraft. The behavior of these vortices is affected by extension of flaps and leading-edge slats, as well as by a change in speed. The FAA says that the basic factor is weight; the vortex strength increases proportionately with aircraft weight. During tests, peak vortex tangential velocities were recorded at 224 feet per second, or

WAKE TURBULENCE

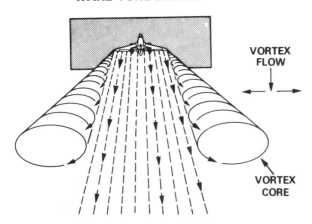

VORTEX
FLOW

VORTEX
CORE

Fig. 2-10. The possibility of encountering wake turbulence can be greatly reduced, ideally eliminated, with proper planning for takeoff and landing around large aircraft. Perhaps a wake turbulence review should be part of every pretakeoff and prelanding checklist.

Fig. 2-11. When departing after the arrival of a large aircraft, rotate after the large aircraft's touchdown point to avoid its wake turbulence after becoming airborne.

about 133 knots. The greatest vortex strength occurs when the generating aircraft is *heavy, clean,* and *slow*.

The vortices, a by-product of lift, begin from the instant the aircraft becomes airborne and cease at the point of touchdown (FIG. 2-11). Vortices close to the ground tend to move laterally at a speed of about four knots, and their movement will be modified by the wind. Because the vortices from heavy airplanes sink at the rate of about 400−500 feet per minute, you must be aware that they can sink into traffic patterns from other operations, or into your aircraft takeoff or landing path from an intersecting runway.

A few simple rules help you stay clear of potential wake turbulence problems:

- If you follow a large or heavy category aircraft on takeoff, lift off prior to its point of rotation, then remain above and upwind of its flight path until you turn clear of its wake.

- Following a large or heavy aircraft on landing, remain at or above its final approach path, and land beyond its touchdown point.

Air traffic tower controllers will provide wake turbulence cautions when they believe it appropriate and will maintain a distance of six miles between a heavy aircraft and a following lightplane landing on the same runway or on a parallel runway fewer than 2,500 feet away.

For takeoff, the separation is a minimum of two minutes or four miles between a heavy aircraft and a following small aircraft from the same runway (a five-mile separation from intersecting runways) and when parallel runways are fewer than 2,500 feet apart.

Note that the takeoff separation is two minutes *or* four miles by radar measurement. You may ask the controller for the two minutes rather than the four miles. On a calm day that might not leave you feeling comfortable about the situation.

Be aware that a helicopter in forward flight produces vortices in its wake similar to vortices created by fixed-wing aircraft.

HURRY-UP APPROACHES

A tower controller might ask you to "expedite" or "make a short approach." *Expedite* means do it *now*; and the directive to *make a short approach* refers to final approach. You might be told to make a straight-in approach, or to enter the pattern on base leg. Gusty conditions can encourage an approach speed higher than the normal 1.3 times stall speed, as can a wind shear warning. Usually, however, the need to hasten an approach is due to the fact that you are sharing the pattern with faster airplanes.

First, let's consider an ATC-directed, straight-in approach. Where should you be, when, and at what speed? Suddenly, you appreciate the stylized pattern with guidelines for everything. You are going to arbitrarily select a starting point or key position from which to set up an approach: two miles from the threshold of the active. You will let down to reach pattern altitude at that point, with your pre-landing chores tidied up.

Initiate the let-down from that point with a reduction in power and lowering of partial flaps. With elevator pressure and trim, adjust airspeed to 60 knots in the Cessna Aerobat (it stalls at 45 knots IAS with flaps and idle power), which translates roughly into two minutes to the runway threshold, depending upon the wind, and that suggests a 500-fpm descent. These are estimates because groundspeed is going to determine actual time to the runway, your two-mile key position was a guess, and you are not going to shoot for the threshold, but about halfway down the first third of the runway.

You can now crank down full flaps, trim off the elevator pressure once again, and watch the intended touchdown point in relation to a fixed reference spot on the windshield in order to determine whether the intended touchdown point moves above or below that reference as the approach progresses.

If the reference spot on the windshield—some instructors make a grease-pencil mark on the windshield—appears to move down in relation to the desired point on the runway, you are going to land short of that point, therefore, add a little power.

If the reference spot on the windshield is moving above the planned touchdown point, you are going to land beyond it, in which case, back off the throttle. Remember, control the rate of descent with power, and control the airspeed with pitch.

If the controller has directed that you enter the pattern on base leg, you should be at pattern altitude when you begin that base, with the threshold approximately 45° off the nose of the airplane. From that point, complete a normal approach. But if this directive is accompanied by a request that you "make a short approach," then fly the base leg so that the turn onto final will be made about 1/4 mile from the threshold.

At controlled airports where there is no congestion, and at uncontrolled airports where there are no special procedures, fly a good standard pattern for plenty of time to concentrate on the landing. It will eliminate the need to catch up with the airplane with last-minute trim and speed corrections. A good final approach distance in single-engine lightplanes under normal conditions is about 1/2 mile, a little longer for retractables.

At uncontrolled airports, a good rule of thumb for lightplane separation is the length of the runway on takeoff, the length of a pattern leg in the pattern, and the decision to go around halfway down final if the active runway is not cleared by then. There will be times when you will get boxed-in between two other planes in the pattern and will need to extend the downwind leg to maintain sufficient approach spacing. The more planes in the pattern, the larger the pattern will grow, but there's not much an individual plane can do about this other than abandoning the pattern and heading to another field.

I haven't gone into detail yet on the use of radios because I agree with those instructors who believe that a student will progress faster and retain more if not overwhelmed with too many new concepts at once. The conventional wisdom among professional educators holds that an instructor should introduce no more than four new concepts or procedures per week to the average student. That is why some flight instructors prefer to wait until their students have absorbed those first few hours of dual instruction before giving them the responsibility of handling the airborne radiotelephone with its special language.

3
Takeoffs

WHAT'S TO KNOW ABOUT TAKEOFFS?" DAUGHTER SANDRA ASKED. "I've watched. All you have to do is give it the gas and steer, right?"

She was only 12 years old at the time so I didn't take her assessment too seriously. "It takes a lot of body English," I said, silently, resolving to volunteer no more words of aeronautical wisdom to my blasé girl-type child until she had accumulated a few more years.

Actually, there is quite a lot to know about takeoffs, depending upon where you start. Every takeoff, whether for a cross-country flight or a local pleasure hop, must be preceded by a certain amount of planning and checking. The go/no-go decision properly begins and ends with weather considerations, but a host of other factors, also critical to a safe flight, include such things as a preflight inspection of the airplane, a check of its operating systems, and the determination that the pilot is not only qualified by training and experience for the task at hand, but physically fit as well.

Fatigue might be the most common of the physically debilitating threats. To be a pilot is to be a decision maker. Every time you fly you must make a number of decisions, many of which cannot be delayed,

Fig. 3-1. Develop a habit of examining an airplane while walking up to it. This is an ideal time to notice a low shock strut, an area of wrinkled skin, especially around landing gear attach areas, or other abnormalities that might not be noticeable at closer range.

most of which are irrevocable, and some of which ensure your continued good health. Fatigue dilutes the quality of your decisions, and it must be a consideration in preflight planning, especially at night. (The FAA recommends supplemental oxygen above 5,000 feet at night.)

Let us assume now that the go/no-go decision has come up "go," that the flight plan has been filed, and that you are leaving the pilots' lounge to walk to the airplane. Acquire the habit of looking at the airplane as you approach it, so that a low shock strut, area of wrinkled skin, or other abnormality is noted (FIG. 3-1). Also, watch for things lying around, such as tool boxes, step ladders, and fueling equipment, that could be a hazard when taxiing. If your airplane is tied down on an airport where there are several rows of lightplanes, always assume, while moving among them, that *every* propeller is either rotating or will begin rotating at any instant.

HAND PROPPING

I'm sure that you have an effective routine for the preflight inspection, walk around, of your aircraft, so I won't give a detailed account of mine except to mention a few procedures that you might not have encountered so far and could prove useful someday.

Sooner or later you are going to be asked by a pilot to "swing my prop." His aircraft battery is dead, and he wants his engine cranked by the "Armstrong" method. If his airplane is a tri-gear, offer to get in the cockpit and handle the switch while *he* swings the propeller. Tell him that his insurance is probably invalid in case of accident with an "unqualified" party propping the airplane. Besides, there *is* a risk involved—you might be surprised how many serious injuries and fatalities result from propeller accidents each year, with pilots at the top of the list—therefore, it's only proper that the party needing the help either assume the risk himself or have his battery removed and charged.

The risk in hand-propping an airplane is greater with tri-gear machines because of the low thrust line of the engine. When you swing a propeller on a tri-gear, you tend to lunge *into* the prop as you follow-through. It's not as bad on tailwheel airplanes because the prop is at eye level or above and it's easy to step backwards as part of your follow-through motion. If the prop kicks back, it can't bash you.

If the dead battery happens to be in *your* airplane, the proper solution is to have it removed and charged. In cold weather, you can get a jump-start from your automobile if your airplane has a 12-volt system, but this procedure usually doesn't provide enough voltage through your voltage regulator to get your alternator on line (you don't have this problem with the old-style generator system).

If your situation requires a hand start, make sure that you have a pilot or licensed aircraft mechanic at the controls with the parking brake set. Wheel chocks are recommended if they have generous lengths of rope attached so they can be removed from behind the engine. It's best to leave the tail tiedown in place. If you must stand on ice, wet grass, or loose gravel in order to swing the prop, move the airplane. Good footing is absolutely necessary. Also make sure that your prop blast is directed so that it cannot cause damage to other aircraft, cars, etc.

To begin this starting procedure, make sure that the ignition switch is in the OFF position. Then, facing the propeller, rotate it counterclockwise to position the blade on your left, a little above horizontal. Stand close enough to obtain a good hold on the blade, but with *only the tips* of your fingers over the upper edge of the blade. Leaning forward in an unbalanced stance can cause you to fall into the blade as the engine starts.

In the airplane, with the throttle set to the normal start position (about $1/4$- to $1/2$-inch open on a Cessna 150), the ignition (magneto) switch is turned to the BOTH position, and then you pull the blade down rapidly. The best way to ensure that there is no misunderstanding between you and the helper in the airplane is to employ the terms and sequence that were standard back in the days before most airplanes had electric starters:

Hand propper: "Switch Off!" He stands clear and awaits reply.

Pilot in Cockpit: "Switch off!" He must physically touch the switch and confirm that it is off.

The hand propper then positions the prop for the starting attempt:

Hand propper: "Contact!"

Pilot in Cockpit: Turns ignition switch to BOTH position and responds, "Contact!"

Hand propper: Pulls the blade through to start the engine. If the engine does not start, he does *not* return to reposition the propeller for another try until calling, "Switch off!" and receiving that echo from the cockpit.

The procedure is simple and effective. Its purpose is to protect the hand propper.

If the airplane has a propeller spinner, keep in mind while hand propping that the spinner might be used to catch yourself with one hand should you lose your footing and fall toward the propeller as the engine starts.

The spinner is often neglected in the preflight inspection, but it should be checked for security of attachment. Spinners have come off in flight. If there are invisible cracks radiating from the spinner's attach bolts, you probably can feel them by grasping the spinner in both hands and attempting to work it in an eccentric circle.

I'd like to stress the importance of checking the propeller for those textbook "nicks, dents, and scratches." The outer third of propeller blades do almost all the work, so pay particular attention there. Any deep scratch in that area should be called to the attention of a mechanic. It could provide a stress point that could lead to blade failure in flight (FIG. 3-2). You should know that when a prop blade departs the airplane in flight, the vibration is so abrupt and severe that you will be able to turn off the ignition only with the greatest difficulty before the engine shakes itself

Fig. 3-2. The leading edge of this propeller has been substantially filed to smooth out gravel and pebble damage. An A&P should be consulted as soon as possible to ensure safety.

free of its mounts, after which, the airplane will be so out of balance it *cannot* be controlled.

Some years ago at Forth Worth, I saw a propeller blade fail in flight on aerobatic champion Hal Krier's Chipmunk. Krier was inverted at about 200 feet (how's *that* for an emergency?), and the Ranger engine wrenched from its mounts within three or four seconds. Meanwhile, Krier rolled upright and put the Chipmunk on the ground in a left forward slip with the engine hanging between the main wheels, attached to the airplane by its fuel and oil lines, which were teflon, covered with braided steel wire. Krier agreed that he was lucky; strong as they were, those fluid lines certainly would not have held the engine for long.

COCKPIT MANAGEMENT

Let's assume that you've checked the weight-and-balance data and that baggage is stowed within limits of maximum weight and CG. It's not much of a problem with a side-by-side trainer, but you must acquire the habit of checking the load and it's placement within the aircraft. Also, always determine that outside baggage doors are secure before entering the airplane.

You will take aboard the airplane with you the aeronautical charts appropriate to the planned flight, along with notepad and pencil, as well as your air navigation pocket computer, either the old standby E6B-type circular slide rule or electronic. Check the cabin for loose articles that might be tossed about in turbulent air.

There is one other item you should take along that has nothing to do with flying or navigating the airplane, but much to do with future pleasure: Place your 35mm camera, loaded with film for color prints, in a map pocket, glove compartment, or other handy place where it can't be tossed about. Don't complicate things with extra lenses or other gadgets (maybe a yellow filter if you want to shoot clouds). And don't rest the camera on any part of the airframe for in-flight photos; the vibration will blur the results. Much of your shooting will be on the ground: the people you fly with, fellow pilots, and the like. Twenty years from now, you will thank me for this suggestion.

I hope you have, and use, printed pre-start and pre-takeoff checklists—yes, even in a two-place trainer. Read each item aloud and then physically touch or appropriately adjust that switch or control.

PRIMER

Now, about the primer. You should have an accurate mental picture of what goes on inside your airplane's operating systems if you expect to correctly employ them, and this device is one that many pilots do not really understand. Your primer is an atomizer. Its purpose is to inject atomized fuel into the engine's fuel induction system. In carbureted recips, the primer should be needed only for cold engine starts. Pull it out slowly to fill it with gasoline, then push it in quickly to obtain the best atomization of the raw fuel. Liquid in the combustion chambers will not ignite; only the gasoline/air mixture will burn. A cold airplane engine does not need a *richer* mixture in order to start, it needs a mixture that will *ignite*.

The reason that your automobile starts when your airplane won't is mostly due to the unique design of the fuel induction system on the lightplane's opposed, air-cooled engine. In most lightplanes the primer nozzle discharges into the intake manifold, which is routed through the oil sump and then upward through risers to each cylinder. In other words, the fuel/air mixture has a long way to go before it reaches the combustion chamber it is destined for.

When the oil is cold there is not much fuel vapor left by the time it reaches the cylinders, because fuel vaporization is a function of temperature. When the oil is hot it heats the fuel/air mix being drawn through the oil sump, and that aids vaporization. That is one reason external oil preheaters are useful in cold weather. The other reason is that warm oil is ready to flow through the engine's lubricating system immediately upon engine start. Start the engine with cold oil and you have bare metal working against bare metal inside the engine for long seconds before any lubricant film is established, and that subtracts many hours from engine life.

Another primer system found on earlier Continentals is connected directly to the two rear cylinders. It does not work very well. Later versions connect the primer to each cylinder, and this is very effective if you shove the primer handle in hard and obtain good atomization.

There are two time-proven ways to get an airplane started on cold mornings (or following an extended period of inactivity). If your airplane has a key start, leave the ignition in the OFF position while you pull the propeller through by hand and a competent helper simultaneously gives it a shot of primer (remember, pull out the primer handle slowly; shove it in hard). This will preload the cylinders with fuel. Then stand clear of the prop as your helper employs the key start. Depending upon temperature and the degree of vaporization achieved, the engine should start with one to three preloads; more will usually flood it.

If you are flying an airplane with a starter button separate from the ignition switch, you can preload the cylinders with vaporized fuel without the need for a helper. Crank and prime with the ignition switch in the OFF position. Then effect a normal start. Clearly, the trick is to judge the proper amount of primer use.

On fuel-injected engines, regard the electric auxiliary fuel pump as a primer. Hot starts seems to cause the most trouble for pilots of these planes. The usual advice is that, if all else fails, try following the directions in your owner's manual. Other suggestions include an extended coffee break, allowing the airplane time to cool, and pouring cold water on the fuel distributor block to condense what is, after all, a simple old-fashioned vapor lock. The cool-down solution is probably the surest—if you haven't exhausted the battery by the time you decide on it. Progress exacts its price.

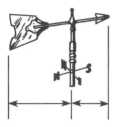 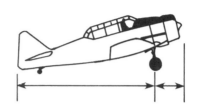 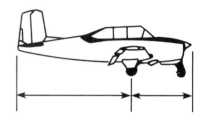

Fig. 3-3. Weathervaning occurs because a greater portion of the aircraft's surface is presented to a crosswind, aft of the main wheels, than the portion of the aircraft's surface that is presented to a crosswind forward of the main wheels. The weathervaning tendency is markedly stronger in tailwheel aircraft.

TAXIING

If you spend much time around an airport, you will arrive at the conclusion that a lot of lightplanes are unnecessarily damaged while moving on the ground. As previously noted, most landing accidents happen on the landing rollout, apparently because pilots tend to consider a flight completed upon touchdown, and begin to turn their attention to other things. Taxiing, before and after a flight, accounts for more careless accidents (FIG. 3-3). Not long ago, I watched helplessly as a pilot taxied his Cherokee toward the parking area, smiling and waving at friends waiting on the apron, and struck the tail of another airplane with his wingtip. As with most taxiing accidents, no one was hurt, but it was expensive. So, the first rule for taxiing an airplane is: Pay attention to the airplane.

Common sense dictates safe taxi speeds. Certain instructors tell their students that taxi speed should not exceed that of a fast walk. The primary requirement is positive control; the ability to stop and turn as desired. Turns should be made slowly and always with the airplane moving forward, if possible; pivoting around a locked brake is hard on tires.

Maintenance-saving habits indirectly contribute to safety and will directly contribute to your pocketbook when you own your own airplane. Fast turns while taxiing impose a strong side-force on the landing gear, and such turns also can set up an uncontrollable swerve that ends in a damaging ground loop. This is especially true as the airplane goes crosswind when turning from downwind to upwind because of its weathervaning tendency (FIG. 3-4).

Rudder pedals are primary directional controls while taxiing. Taxi with your heels on the floor and the balls of your feet low on the rudder pedals. Later, you can rest the arches of your feet on the rudder pedals and toes near the brakes, a position required for simultaneous pressure on

Fig. 3-4. The apron at this airport is 100 yards wide and 200 yards long. Only three other aircraft were in all that space, but the pilot of this Piper managed to taxi the Cherokee into one of them. Pay attention is the first rule to follow when taxiing an aircraft.

the rudder and brake when needed. You will sometimes find it handy to use differential braking to help maintain a straight track in a crosswind landing rollout or during taxi on an icy surface. You can get a little help from flight controls when taxiing in significant wind; in a crosswind, use full up-aileron into the wind.

Certain pilots will argue that flight controls are ineffective at speeds below 30−35 knots and that you have no business operating a lightplane in a crosswind component of 30 knots or more. Theoretically, that's correct; however, sometimes terrain- or obstacle-induced turbulence or gusts are present, or the crosswind component is stronger than anticipated. When judging a personal wind limit, your major concerns are the crosswind and tailwind you have to contend with while taxiing. Taking off into a 20-knot headwind is no problem, but getting to the takeoff position might be.

NORMAL TAKEOFF

I hope you don't weary of my repeated mention of your aircraft owner's manual. It's important that you reference it for a number of things, including liftoff and climb speeds under varying conditions. That is where you obtain the base numbers with which to establish the amount of takeoff run at various altitudes, temperatures, and aircraft weights. You have to add your own fudge factors for runway slope and conditions, plus another 10 percent for the wife and kids. It won't always be exact, but it's a lot better than the "grit-yer-teeth-and-hope" method.

Most of the data are directly applicable without interpolation. It's true that the book figures were established with a new airplane flown by a professional test pilot, but those performance figures are for max gross weight and while the manufacturer has a little cushion in those recommended figures, time takes its toll on aircraft performance so that, on balance, it's still a good idea to add that extra 10 percent to all estimated takeoff requirements.

Having taxied into position on the taxiway just short of the runway (behind the double line), perform the pre-takeoff check, reading aloud each item on the printed list (the checklists are sometimes mounted on the instrument panel) and replying aloud as you touch or adjust that control. For example, "Carburetor heat." Touch the knob, look at its position, and reply, "Cold," and the like.

You might have set the altimeter to local conditions before you started to taxi of you caught the ATIS broadcast, or Tower (or Ground Control at large airports) will supply the altimeter setting, along with wind, temperature, and taxi instructions. If flying from an uncontrolled airport, the field elevation should be painted on a sign beside the taxiway. If it's not visible, you can always take it from the sectional chart.

I'll not detail the pre-takeoff checks except to mention that you should swing the airplane in a complete circle to get an unobstructed view of the entire traffic pattern at uncontrolled airports. Also at uncontrolled fields, you will be transmitting your position and intentions on the CTAF and, of course, monitoring that frequency for the transmissions of other responsible citizens.

Set the directional gyro (DG) to conform with the runway's magnetic bearing. If you don't have an operating DG, you'll have to do it the old-fashioned way: select distant references that you can use to maintain a straight track during the takeoff run and initial climbout (FIG. 3-5). Usually, of course, you have the runway centerline for takeoff reference. On grass you will have to use trees, mountains, smokestacks, or something else.

There is no valid reason to take off using less than full power. The air-cooled lightplane engine is designed to operate at full throttle (unless otherwise placarded). As long as the needles of the engine gauges remain

Fig. 3-5. Thousands of instructors have told thousands of students: "Track straight out along the extended runway centerline." The runway is almost hidden by the 150's rudder.

in the green arcs, the engine is not being overworked.

Save your concern for a component that needs to be babied a little—the odd wheel of your landing gear, for example. Whether under the nose or under the tail, the third wheel on lightplanes is the most bothersome, both in maintenance and in operation. On takeoff in a tri-gear, unless you have a crosswind to contend with, most instructors will tell you to hold no more forward pressure on the control wheel than is necessary for positive steering. This may mean no forward pressure at all.

The key is proper trim. Then you can usually allow the elevators to trail naturally in the slipstream, the object being to lighten the nosewheel as soon as is practicable while still maintaining the airplane in a minimum drag configuration for efficient acceleration. Except in extreme circumstances, avoid the use of differential braking on takeoff because that can throw you into an uncontrollable swerve. It also, of course, prolongs the takeoff roll.

The best takeoff attitude is close to the airplane's best rate-of-climb attitude. It takes only a small amount of back pressure on the control wheel. You can do this better by feel than by the numbers, which is why you normally establish a liftoff attitude and let the airplane fly itself off. There are exceptions; some airplanes simply have to be lifted off. You'll do them by feel also. The actual airspeed will usually be at least 10 percent over stalling speed in that configuration and weight, but this can vary; a number of factors can influence your procedure, including runway condition, slope, density altitude, and turbulence.

CROSSWIND TAKEOFF

The crosswind takeoff differs from a normal takeoff in two distinct ways: You will hold aileron into the wind, and you should add five knots to your liftoff speed. At the beginning of the takeoff run, full up-aileron into the wind is not going to have much effect. The ailerons are the last flight controls to become effective because they are outside the propeller slipstream. Maintain a straight track with rudder, as always. However, you may have to hold *downwind* rudder pressure because, on the ground, the airplane (especially tailwheel airplanes) will tend to weathervane. A crosswind from the right might be sufficient to counteract torque, which yaws the airplane to the left. A wind from the left will aggravate the air-

Fig. 3-6. When the nosewheel lifts off, the aileron into the slight crosswind might cause the downward wing to rise and the downwind main wheel to leave the runway first.

plane's left-turning tendency at full power. Use whatever rudder is called for to maintain a straight track down the centerline. The amount of aileron needed will gradually diminish as the ailerons become more effective with increasing speed (FIG. 3-6).

You want that extra five knots at liftoff because you leave the ground in an instant slip into the wind, and you don't want to take a chance that a gust or turbulence will put you back on the ground, however briefly, moving sideways. You may hold the slip into the wind during initial climb, or you can establish a crab with wings level and retrim after the climbout is set up.

SHORT-FIELD TAKEOFF

The owner's manuals for some airplanes recommend up to 25° or flaps for short-field takeoffs. The owner's manual for a Cessna trainer recommends no flaps. In any case, this is a maximum performance takeoff (FIG. 3-7), and in a fixed-gear trainer the main difference between a short-field takeoff and a normal takeoff is liftoff and initial climb at best-angle-of-climb airspeed V_x. Once clear of all obstacles, change to best-rate-of-climb speed, V_y. Here is where your slow flight practice helps justify the effort you invested in it. V_x leaves you with little margin for error and requires careful airspeed control.

Takeoff from a short field requires that you use all of the field that is available, and that you accelerate as fast as you can. Years ago, the recommended procedure was to hold brakes (or lacking brakes, have helpers hold the wings) while the throttle was opened to maximum. When the rpm reached peak, brakes were released. When tests showed that this method didn't seem to shorten the takeoff run appreciably, pilots were told to release the brakes and smoothly open the throttle like a normal takeoff. Now it's back to hold the brakes while you call on the engine for max power, the explanation being that you need to check the mags while the engine is going full bore to make certain that you are going to have maximum power when the brakes are released.

Clearly, you will achieve maximum acceleration by the common sense procedure of presenting the least possible resistance to the air—meaning that you will hold the flight controls in neutral and roll with zero angle of attack—and, if you have any choice, use the ground that offers the least impediment to your wheels. Too often, the short field is also a soft and/or rough field. As a general rule, flap settings of 30° or less produce more lift than drag, but the use of flaps on takeoff also subtracts from acceleration. To get something, you have to give something. While

Fig. 3-7. A short-field takeoff in a Debonair with 10 degrees of flaps is demonstrated by Beech Aircraft Corporation pilot Larry Ball. He held the brakes and applied full throttle prior to releasing the brakes and initiating the short-field takeoff roll.

you are told to use no flaps for a short-field takeoff in the Cessna trainer, the owner's manual for the Piper Cherokee says to use them.

In tailwheel airplanes, you want to get the tailwheel off the ground and the aircraft in level attitude for maximum acceleration during the takeoff roll. Some instructors recommend a tail-low attitude for tailwheel airplanes during the short-field takeoff run because, they say, that allows the airplane to fly off as soon as it is ready, which is obviously true.

Which procedure gets you off the ground quicker with good control? Certainly the latter technique might be dictated for a tri-gear airplane if the short field is also soft, so that your short-field technique becomes more of a soft-field technique. In other words, the short-field takeoff procedure puts emphasis on acceleration, while the soft-field procedure emphasizes getting airborne quickly. There is a difference because you can get off the ground at an airspeed that is insufficient to take you out of ground effect.

SOFT-FIELD TAKEOFF

Takeoff from a soft field—mud, sand, snow, tall grass, or any surface that retards the takeoff run—is primarily a question of attaining liftoff as quickly as possible, while seeking every ounce of lift you can muster from the instant the wheels begin to roll. Unless you are flying a T-tail, elevators are in the propeller slipstream and working in slightly compressed air due to their proximity to the surface and are the first flight controls to become effective, allowing you to assume a positive angle of attack soon after you begin to roll. The immediate objective is to get the nosewheel out of the mush. The nose-high attitude, not too high, about the same as the normal liftoff attitude, will result in a progressive transfer of weight from the mains to the wings during acceleration.

Theoretically, the slightly nose-high attitude increases drag—remember, drag is a by-product of lift—and subtracts from acceleration, but lift is the first concern, and you'll accept it at whatever speed gets a few inches of daylight between the mains and the surface. Level off in ground effect, being careful not to push the wheels back into the slush or whatever, and then accelerate to V_x if there are obstacles to be cleared, to V_y if practicable.

Someone is certain to advise you to get a "running start" if a little bit of firm surface is available, but that can be risky because even a fast taxi speed from a smooth hard surface to a rough soft one will most likely cause your nosewheel to dig a hole, whether it is off the ground or not.

The situation can be equally risky if you try to make a high-speed *turn* into the takeoff area after accelerating from a more desirable surface. That might place an unacceptable side load on the landing gear, and it can, if the fuel cell in use is less than half full and not well-baffled inside, force fuel away from the pick-up in the cell, resulting in momentary fuel starvation at a most inopportune time.

THIN AIR

High-altitude takeoffs require more *true* airspeed than you are likely to suspect if all your flying has been from fields below, say 1,500 feet msl. When density altitude is near 11,000 feet, which is not too unusual at Santa Fe or Albuquerque on a summer afternoon (85−90 °F), 70 knots indicated is about 87 knots true, and under such conditions if you lift off at the normal 48 to 50 knots indicated, the true airspeed is about 62 knots, which is visually quite apparent as the takeoff roll progresses.

So, do not allow that obvious speed to influence liftoff; reference only the airspeed indicator, an indication reinforced by your *aerodynamic* feel of the machine. Your takeoff roll will be long, and you'll be rolling at a high ground speed. Be prepared, and lift off at the normal IAS unless there are obstacles or other considerations to modify your technique.

Fig. 3-8. The denalt pocket computer provides takeoff distance and rate of climb at various altitudes and temperatures. Instructions are printed on the face. There are separate versions for fixed-pitch and variable-pitch propeller installations. Density altitude can also be computed with one of several aviation pocket calculators on the market.

Because temperature is a controlling factor in the determination of density altitude, high-altitude takeoffs during warm weather are often planned for the relatively cooler morning hours (FIGS. 3-8 through 3-10). Such planning beats the winds that are generated by convection activity, and also avoids the thunderstorms that are an almost daily occurrence in the mountains from midday onward in the summertime.

Taking off from an airport with a density altitude of 5,000 feet or greater, flying a normally aspirated engine (not turbocharged), you should lean the fuel mixture or else suffer a loss in performance from an engine that is already operating at least 15° below its rated power. There is a small problem with this. You will be guessing, because you'll be leaning the fuel mixture at magneto-check rpm of 1,700, meaning that you have adjusted the mixture for that engine speed. Pull out the mixture knob until the engine begins to run rough, then push in the mixture to smooth out the engine, perhaps giving it an extra quarter-inch to keep the cylinder heads cool. After takeoff, with your climb established, you may readjust the mixture for the higher power setting.

Fig. 3-9. Typical takeoff chart for various density altitudes as given in an aircraft owner's handbook.

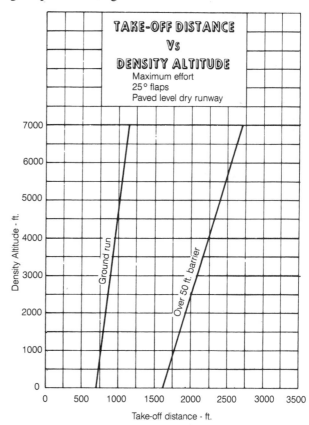

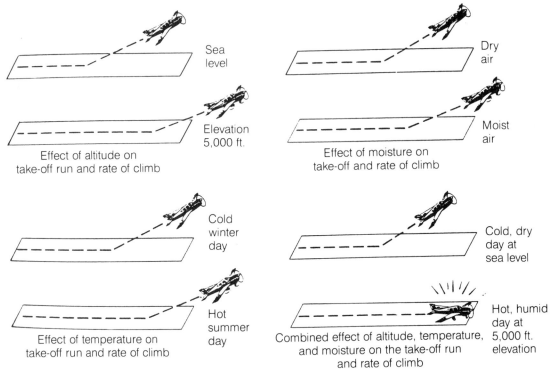

Effect of altitude on
take-off run and rate of climb

Effect of moisture on
take-off and rate of climb

Effect of temperature on
take-off run and rate of climb

Combined effect of altitude, temperature,
and moisture on the take-off run
and rate of climb

Fig. 3-10. Many changeable factors affect aircraft takeoff performance.

This procedure is not very precise. The best way to do it is by reference to an *exhaust gas temperature* (EGT) gauge, along with oil and cylinder-head temperature gauges. Leaning the fuel mixture with an EGT provides a reference point, or peak temperature of the exhaust, which is the temperature of most complete combustion. Pull out the mixture control until EGT peaks, then enrich to about 150° on the rich side of peak; the extra fuel is a coolant, which is why air-cooled engines are not as fuel efficient as liquid-cooled engines. Monitor cylinder-head and oil temperatures. If they climb out of the green arcs, enrichen the mixture.

As a practical matter, climbout after takeoff from a high-altitude airport will often be what the conditions (density altitude, winds, surrounding terrain) allow. If there are obstacles to surmount, tall trees, sharply rising terrain, or the like, a check of your owner's manual prior to takeoff should reveal that your best-angle-of-climb speed increases with altitude, while your best-rate-of-climb speed drops. The manufacturer's engineering test pilots went to a lot of trouble to draw the graphs and compile the tables in the owner's manual; use those data. And add 10 percent, because it's unlikely that you will get the same performance from the airplane that they did.

A common problem at high-altitude airports is engine overheating due to prolonged operation on the ground before takeoff. At idle and taxi speeds you don't have the volume of air flowing around the cylinder that they receive down in the flatlands.

WET AND ICY

A takeoff might be questionable when a third or more of the runway is covered by as little as $1/2$ inch of water, wet snow, or slush. I don't mean a third of the runway all at one end—you probably can avoid that. What I'm talking about here are patches of such stuff. Each time you hit a patch of slush it's analogous to a sudden application of brakes. Approaching takeoff velocity and plowing into a large puddle of water or patch of slush might slam the nosewheel into the mush with enough force to damage that vulnerable component and/or start a severe swerve, the latter especially when one main hits the slush and one does not.

Lesser depths of water or wet snow might be overcome, although you must add up to 20 percent to your normal takeoff run. Common sense is really the final guide, and it's probably worth the effort to select an accelerate/stop point along the runway where, if you have not attained liftoff velocity, it's time to shut down and abort the takeoff. Selecting the accelerate/stop point is not hard if you have equally spaced runway lights to use in determining distance or if you use a taxiway of known distance from the threshold. Consult your owner's manual for the takeoff distance required in the prevailing density altitude conditions and add 20 percent to that for surface conditions. Then ask yourself if there is room enough to stop beyond your accelerate/stop point.

In cold weather, water or slush on the runway, even in small amounts, can be splashed into the wheel wells of retractables and packed into the wheel pants of fixed-gear airplanes, there to freeze in the colder air aloft after takeoff. I don't need to tell you about the interesting events to follow when it comes time to lower the gear and land. Leave the gear down following takeoff until the wheel wells are dried. The only way to ensure that wheels do not freeze inside tight-fitting wheel pants is to remove the pants for the winter.

A refreeze danger is also present when an ice-covered airplane that has been tied down out-of-doors is rolled into a heated hangar to prepare it for flight. Ice and snow that have melted and drained into surface wells and hinges can refreeze during or following takeoff and interfere with the

Fig. 3-11. A refreeze hazard occurs when an ice-covered airplane is rolled into a heated hangar for flight preparations. Melted ice, frost, or snow can drain into control surface wells, or into the flight controls themselves, and refreeze in the outside air. Ethylene glycol, if applied hot, is the best ice remover, but its effectiveness is questionable if applied cold. This twin-engine Champion Lancer has a bit wider margin of safety for winter operations, compared to single-engine airplanes.

operation of the flight controls at a critical time. Pay particular attention to control surface drain/ventilation holes to make sure that trapped water does not remain inside an elevator or aileron to freeze later in flight resulting in imbalance and flutter that could lead to failure (FIGS. 3-11 and 3-12).

Soft-field techniques are best in almost all snow and slush conditions. If the snow is too deep to allow the airplane to accelerate, you can sometimes make several runs down the same tracks to pack the snow, but there is nothing you can do with slush or water when there is enough of it to impede your takeoff run.

In areas where the snow lasts all winter, some lightplane pilots switch to skis during the cold months rather than place the airplane in storage until spring. That kind of flying is different enough to require a checkout by an experienced skiplane instructor. There are other considerations, not

Fig. 3-12. Even a light coating of frost significantly increases an air-plane's stalling speed; it's not the additional weight, but the drag that creates the problem.

the least of which is where the airplane is parked. If you have ever tried to open T-hangar doors with bottom rollers encased in a couple of inches of ice, or if you have asked yourself what you were doing on a snow-covered deserted airport contemplating an engine pre-heater rendered useless of a dead electrical outlet, you might have decided that winter storage for your personal airplane isn't such a dumb idea after all.

DUST DEVILS

Elements of nature, primarily air, permit man to fly, and one relatively rare element of nature can disrupt any light aircraft. Dust devils appear harmless enough when seen while driving through the country-side. A small one merely whips around leaves and trash. A healthy dust devil can rise to unexpected heights and carry enough dust to become opaque and resemble a tornado without a cloud.

If the whirlwind happens to cross a road as you pass in the car, the vehicle might be buffeted by the blast, which might dissipate after colliding with the car. Encountering a dust devil while in an automobile and encountering a dust devil while in an aircraft are two entirely different situations.

Witnessed

An ideal summer day beckoned a pilot to shoot touch-and-gos in the afternoon. The wind sock and tetrahedron indicated that the wind speed was moderate from the north, which was straight down the runway. Two or three aircraft were in the pattern at any one time. Fortunately, the pilot's flying club's Grumman American Cheetah was available. It was shaping up to be a great day for flying.

The pilot pulled the Cheetah out of the hangar and performed his usual extremely thorough preflight because he believed the inspection was an excellent way to simultaneously prepare aircraft and pilot for flight. Unicom was fairly busy with traffic reports from aircraft in the pattern, and he did not rush to the end of the runway for the run-up. The end of the runway was so far away from the hangars that many pilots opted to perform run-ups on a clean concrete pad near the hangars and close to the FBO because it would be quicker to taxi to the FBO for assistance, if needed. Today the pilot opted to run-up on the concrete pad; the aircraft was ready and he thought that he was ready, but observing another aircraft on final approach made him think twice.

The active runway laid to the right of the taxiway, and a 172 passed just as it became airborne. A Beechcraft Sundowner's pilot announced takeoff intentions and moved onto the runway. The Cheetah pilot scanned the approach end of the runway and spotted a familiar aircraft. A Cessna 120 that was commonly flown by any one of several airport employees was on final approach. The Sundowner was airborne and passed the taxiing Cheetah and the runway was clear, which should have permitted the Cessna 120 to land without incident.

Something caught the eye of the Cheetah pilot. Debris was whirling around approximately 20 to 30 yards away from the right side of the runway numbers (the left side for approaching aircraft). A quick glance revealed that the debris was swirling at the base of a dust devil that appeared to rise 30 or 40 feet. The Cessna 120 was on a short final to landing. The dust devil was a short distance from intersecting the runway.

The Cheetah pilot hoped that the Cessna 120 pilot had seen the dust devil; the Cessna had no transceiver, which prevented any last minute warning on unicom. Also, hopefully, the dust devil might harmlessly pass over the runway, clear of the Cessna 120. Hoping did not help.

The Cessna was starting to flair, approximately 10 to 15 feet above the runway when it encountered the dust devil. One wing dipped and the aircraft yawed in the midst of the dust; the nose pitched down and the tail started to rise just before the pilot got ahead of the dust devil's control of the Cessna. The prompt recovery leveled the Cessna's wings and miraculously it was still heading down the runway for a subsequent successful landing without a go-around.

This episode caused the Cheetah pilot to pause at the end of the runway and consider the lesson. He decided to add whirlwinds to his scan prior to takeoff and landing, for his own protection. For the protection of others, he decided to make radio reports of any whirlwind sighting for the benefit of any pilot flying an aircraft equipped with a transceiver.

4
Over the Fence

THE FINAL APPROACH IS AS MUCH A PART OF THE LANDING AS IT is a part of the airport traffic pattern. That's what flight instructors mean when they say, "Good landings start with good approaches."

In a sense, the downwind and base legs are also parts of the landing. On downwind, which is flown at normal cruising speed, apply carburetor heat and take a good look at the airport in general, the active runway in particular, and any taxiing aircraft that might need watching. (I once had a Continental Airlines Convair swing onto the runway and take off at then-uncontrolled Lawton, Oklahoma, Municipal Airport as I was turning final in a Luscombe with a failed engine. I remember wishing aloud that he would bust his next physical.)

On the downwind leg, be conscious of the runway's position parallel to your flight path and use it to detect any drifting toward or away from it. Precision, remember?

Any wind effect that you notice at initial pattern altitude is not necessarily duplicated on the surface, but it can be a clue. Wind usually increases with altitude, and normally "backs" to come from a more westerly direction.

As the runway threshold passes the left wingtip (assuming a left-hand pattern), reduce power and adjust the fuel mixture to the full rich position. On a Cessna trainer, 10° of flaps is optional at this point as the airspeed permits flap deployment. Later, as you move up to more complex aircraft, there will be more to do. You will have a pre-landing checklist that includes a booster pump, and a wastegate to open (on turbocharged engines), along with propeller pitch control, which goes to high rpm setting after the airplane has slowed to its approach speed.

When the runway threshold appears to be about 45° behind the left wing, make your turn to base leg. Leveling the wings on base, you can further reduce power if necessary, and hold the nose up with elevator until your airspeed slows to near final approach speed. You'll need a bit of left rudder to counteract the decrease in torque. Nearing final approach speed (60−65 knots in a typical trainer), add another notch of flaps and maintain the desired speed with pitch. Speed control is the key to a good approach. Most pilots carry too much airspeed down final. The figures given in the owner's manual are predicated on maximum gross weight; yet you seldom land at that weight. With the airspeed stabilized, retrim, and don't forget your complete scan. Particularly, look off the outside wing for any aircraft that might be making a long final. At uncontrolled airports, commuter airlines like to make such approaches.

The turn to the final approach leg is a descending turn with a shallow bank—repeat, *shallow*, like 30° in smooth air; perhaps 15° in turbulence (FIG. 4-1). You will probably have to "play" this turn to compensate for any wind that is not directly down the runway. Your immediate objective, of course, is to line up with the runway centerline. Wait until you are sure that you can reach the runway before lowering full flaps. Flaps will significantly increase the angle of descent, and it is best not to deploy full flaps too soon because once they are down, retracting them to stretch an approach can be dangerous. You should only stretch the approach with throttle.

In fact, it is unlikely that you will be able to continue a landing approach with power at idle unless there is no wind. A stabilized power setting down final might be desired, but in most cases a number of things intrude that require an increase or decrease in the power setting to adjust your rate of descent. With your touchdown spot matched to a spot on your windshield, you keep it there with light touches of power or power reduction.

If wind is drifting the aircraft to one side or the other of the runway centerline (FIG. 4-2), drop the appropriate wing into the wind with aileron, while maintaining a straight track down the centerline with opposite rudder. This is, of course, a very gentle, prolonged slip. Maintain air-

Fig. 4-1. Turning from base leg to final approach at an airport using a right-hand pattern. The runway threshold is approximately 3/4 mile away, and the aircraft altitude is approximately 700 feet above the ground.

speed with pitch and rate of descent with power as usual. However, if the crosswind component requires that you carry the upwind wing quite low, you might not have enough rudder to keep the airplane's longitudinal axis aligned with the runway's centerline as speed erodes during the flare. Therefore, if you've got the upwind wing down pretty far and a lot of rudder is needed to maintain track, consider going around and landing on a different runway—even if it means going to another airport.

At controlled airports, you will have the surface wind conditions from the tower or ATIS, and your owner's manual will list the maximum allowable crosswind, which is one of the numbers you should know before flying. Allow a little for gusts, your experience level, and the condition of your airplane (the numbers in the owner's manual were established by a highly competent test pilot flying a brand-new airplane at gross weight in *standard atmosphere conditions*, that is, corrected to sea level and 59 °F, unless otherwise noted).

At uncontrolled airports you are forced to judge the surface wind from the appearance of the windsock and whatever other clues you can observe. As a rule, you shouldn't place too much faith in unicom weather observations. I will discuss crosswind landings in more detail momentarily.

Fig. 4-2. Line up with the runway centerline, but wait until landing on the runway is assured before lowering full flaps. In this instance, the aircraft is slightly to the right of the centerline and slightly low. A touch of power will put everything back on track.

FORWARD SLIPS

Back in the open-cockpit biplane days, fliers had neither flaps nor any suspicion that they needed them. On final approach, they performed *forward slips* to shed excess altitude without picking up unwanted airspeed. The hot pilots often slipped both ways. Wing flaps have proven a lot more practical and, surely, safer. There is, however, still a need to master the forward slip. I can be a real lifesaver if you ever have to shoehorn the aircraft into a small field somewhere with a failed engine. And you must be able to demonstrate an acceptable forward slip on flight tests.

The slip is a simple maneuver, but it contains a possible danger for the unwary. During a slip the relative wind is entering the pitot head at an angle and the airspeed indicator is not giving an accurate reading. So the slip is, to a great extent, a seat-of-the-pants maneuver. Simply lower a wing in the direction of the slip (with aileron) and apply opposite rudder. The longitudinal axis of the airplane is yawed at an angle to the runway centerline, but the ground track remains aligned with the centerline. The amount of rudder needed will vary with the bank angle.

Exactly where along the approach the slip is established will depend upon the situation. Unfortunately, pilots often wait until the need is unmistakable, usually on short final. Termination of the slip is also a judgment call. Don't overdo this maneuver. If a moderate slip is not sufficient, it's time to think about a go-around. The belated need for a forward slip is in itself a good indication of poor planning; don't attempt to salvage a poorly planned approach.

In a slip, the wings lose significant lift because of the change in relative wind; this results in a loss of altitude. But, because of the extra drag produced by the airplane's sideways attitude, the airplane does not pick up airspeed. Meanwhile, you must hold some back pressure on the control wheel to prevent airspeed from increasing.

As I said, it is a seat-of-the pants maneuver, and you can see where the danger lurks for inexperienced pilots. You enter the slip from approach airspeed, you are close to the ground, your controls are crossed, you are holding the nose up with the elevator, and you are referencing an uncertain airspeed indicator. Good grief. . . .

Actually, it isn't as bad as it sounds, because you are only a couple of seconds from returning the airplane to its normal approach configuration. To do this, simultaneously level the wings and return the rudder to neutral. Continue to hold a little back pressure on the control wheel as required for airspeed control. The secret of a good slip is to hold just the right amount of up-elevator to keep the nose from dropping. Too much, of course, could stall the airplane.

Never slip in gusty wind conditions or over approach terrain that could generate orographic turbulence. Check the airplane's owner's manual for any prohibition of slips, including slips with flaps deployed. For years, pilots were told they must not slip a Cessna trainer with flaps down. Cessna later changed that to say it was "not recommended." Flap travel is limited to 30° on late-model Cessna 152s, and slips are acceptable.

RETURN TO EARTH

Don't hurry the flare (FIG. 4-3 through 4-5). Up to this point you have accomplished two-thirds of the landing; the rest is going to fall into place if you have done everything right so far. As you reach the height above the runway where the flare is begun (a good estimate is one-half the plane's wingspan, or 12 to 15 feet in a light single-engine airplane), start to apply back pressure on the control wheel to further slow the airplane. Do this as slowly and steadily as possible. In practice, you can judge when to start the flare by looking as far ahead as you would if driving a car at the same speed. If you look too far down the runway, you will have a tendency to flare too late and too low. If you don't look far enough down the runway, or look to the side, you will tend to flare too high.

Fig. 4-3. This is a controlled airport, and controllers appreciate pilots who safely expedite a takeoff or landing, especially when things get busy. In this instance, the aircraft is slightly high and probably will not land in time to make the first exit; the pilot should not dive the aircraft down to the runway, merely let the aircraft roll after touchdown and catch the next taxiway.

Fig. 4-4. Focus well ahead of the airplane, perhaps on the end of the runway, during the flare.

Fig. 4-5. A proper flair paves the way for a smooth landing.

Power should be at idle when you begin the flare. What you are trying to do is hold the airplane off the runway as long as you possibly can with pitch alone. Expect to run out of up-elevator travel as the airplane stalls at about one foot above the surface. If you see that you are going to stall while still several feet in the air, release a little back pressure. If you are settling too fast, feed in a touch of power, but make no large control or power changes; it takes a light touch here. If you feel the mains touch before the control wheel is all the way back, do not yank the wheel back to catch up; merely continue to smoothly and steadily bring it on back to the stops.

A precipitous decrease in pitch as the airplane settles those final few feet will almost certainly result in a bounce, the severity of which will depend upon the sink rate. Do not attempt to correct a bounce by shoving the control wheel forward. Just feed in a touch of power, keep the nose high because you don't want the nosewheel to touch first, and allow to settle gently.

With the mains rolling, maintain a straight track down the runway centerline with the rudder, and hold the nosewheel off as long as possible. As speed dissipates, the nosewheel will gently lower on its own accord. Do not use brakes until the nosewheel is down. There are several advantages in doing it this way when conditions permit.

1. With the nose high, you are getting effective aerodynamic braking from the wings during the first third of the rollout, thereby reducing brake wear.

2. You are saving wear on the nosewheel tire and the rather weak—and expensive—nosewheel shimmy dampener on Cessnas.

3. You are relieving a good deal of stress on the nose gear attach points.

Even though you might not be directly paying for the maintenance on a training airplane, the day might come when you own an airplane, so maintenance-saving habits are useful to acquire.

The full-stall landing is also easier on the main landing gear and tires. All those black tire marks on the first third of the runway are spin-up marks, put down during the split-second of main-gear touchdown, when tire rotation accelerates from zero to touchdown velocity. You not only leave a little rubber on the concrete every time you land, but you also place a significant rearward force on the landing gear struts and their attachment areas. Lightplanes are normally designed to withstand a rearward force on their main gear that is 20 percent greater than that imposed when touching down at stall speed. Land faster than that and you risk permanent distortion of the landing gear attachment area. On the other hand, you can drop the airplane onto the runway from two or three feet in a full-stall landing without damaging the structure.

Many pilots like to raise the flaps as soon as the main wheels are on the runway in order to decrease lift, transfer weight to the wheels, and improve the ground steering ability after the nosewheel comes down. But most instructors seem to frown on this practice. They say that it's easy to fumble around and grab the wrong control, perhaps raising the landing gear instead of the flaps, when your attention is required outside of the cockpit during rollout. They maintain this belief despite the fact that most flap controls are shaped like a flap and most landing gear controls are shaped like a wheel. The problem, of course, is Murphy's Law, said to have been promulgated by the pilot of the first retractable-gear airplane in 1921.

As speed dissipates during the landing rollout, remain alert and sensitive to any tendency of the airplane to deviate from its straight track. Many aircraft have been bent on landing rollout because pilots simply "quit payin' attention." Remember the ancient and hallowed saying: "You are flying it until it's in the hangar."

VISUAL APPROACH SLOPE INDICATOR

Many airports have a visual approach slope indicator (VASI), a system of lights located near the runway threshold, usually on the left side, sometimes on both sides, that provides pilots with a visual glide-slope reference to maintain a safe and proper glide path. They provide safe obstruction clearance within $\pm 10°$ of the extended runway centerline, and up to 4 nm from the runway threshold. Two-bar VASIs give light-planes a three-degree approach path. Three-bar installations serve light-planes with the closest set of lights and airliners with the middle and far sets of lights to compensate for the higher cockpits. Some VASI installations have glide slopes of up to $4^{1}/2°$ for safe obstacle clearance.

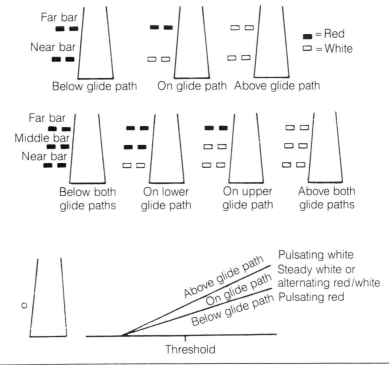

Caution: When viewing the pulsating visual approach slope indicators in the pulsating white or pulsating red sectors, it is possible to mistake this lighting aid for another aircraft or a ground vehicle. Pilots should exercise caution when using this type of system.

Fig. 4-6. The visual approach slope indicator (VASI) system is perhaps the best piece of safety equipment on any airport: top, two-bar; middle, three-bar; and, bottom, pulsating.

The basic principle of these systems is color differentiation between red and white. Each light projects a beam with a white segment in the upper part and a red segment in the lower part of the beam. Red above and white below means that you are on the glide path, all red indicates that you are too low, and all white means that you are too high.

Other types of visual approach slope systems are based on a single light unit. One of these is tri-color: amber if you are above the glide path, red if you are below, and green if you are on the glide path. Dark amber might appear momentarily when the color changes from green to red.

Another is a single-light unit that shows pulsating white when high, pulsating red when low, and a steady white or alternating red-and-white when on the glide path. This rather rare system can be mistaken for another airplane or ground vehicle at night, so use caution.

There is also a low-cost and very dependable system that consists of three plywood panels, usually painted black and white, or international orange (FIG. 4-6). To use this system, position the airplane so that the panels appear to be in lateral alignment (the center one is actually set behind the other two). If you are too high, the center panel will show "above" or farther away; if too low, the center panel will appear closer or "below" the other two. All such systems are pictured and described in detail in the *Airman's Information Manual*.

ABORTED LANDINGS

Any number of things can dictate a balked landing; a final approach that is too high, spacing that is too tight, or an impossible directive from a controller. Final approach isn't the place to argue with a controller. Just say to him, "Tower, Cessna Two Seven Juliet. Unable to comply. Going around."

If Tower doesn't then give you specific instructions for a go-around, the procedure you will follow depends upon where you are in the pattern. You are completely within your rights to reject any ATC directive that could create a dangerous situation for you, is beyond your ability or experience level, or exceeds the capability of your aircraft. If you are flying a Cessna 172 and Approach Control or Tower has sequenced you into the pattern ahead of a Learjet and then admonishes you to speed up, use common sense. Accommodate the bizjet and the controller to the extent that you safely can, but don't allow them to stampede you into a risky procedure. It may be possible for you to whistle over the fence at near double your normal approach speed and, if there is enough runway, smoke your binders to a stop before plowing through the opposite fence, but it is hardly sensible. Your commonsense options, if you believe that you cannot significantly increase your speed and then land safely, are to let the jet go around while you complete your landing, or you may opt to go around instead, not because you are chicken, but as an act of courtesy. Perhaps you have noticed how, in the operation of various aircraft, that courtesy and safety go together.

The need to abort a landing usually becomes impossible to ignore by the time you are on short final. There is a temptation to postpone such a decision as long as possible, but good airmanship demands an early decision. The sooner you decide, the easier and safer it will be.

Assuming that you are on short final, with full flaps and partial power, apply full power and turn off the carburetor heat. Bring up the flaps to the setting recommended for go-around in the owner's manual, usually the same as for a soft-field takeoff, which is 10° in the Cessna 150/152, but raise the flaps in 10-degree increments. Raising flaps reduces lift, so don't bring them up all at once. With the aircraft in level attitude, briefly hold what you have until you pick up speed and retrim, then establish a climb in the normal manner; hold level flight as speed builds and while you retrim, then climb out at V_y or V_x (best rate or best angle) as conditions indicate. Turn onto the crosswind leg of the pattern, carefully scanning for other traffic.

Remember that power is your first consideration, and be prepared to counter the torque with rudder as you feed in full throttle. And if traffic is taking off from the runway below, fly to the right of, and parallel to, the runway so you can keep an eye on the traffic.

If a go-around is called for by a horrific bounce, the result of flaring too high or perhaps not flaring at all, just remain calm, apply full power, ease forward on the wheel to level flight attitude, carb heat to the cold position, and slowly bring the flaps up to the manufacturer's recommended setting for a go-around. You'll have to correct for torque, retrim, and inform the controller of your intentions.

It isn't likely that you will find it necessary to abort a landing from the downwind or base leg of an airport traffic pattern, but it does happen, usually because someone does something dumb. If pattern traffic is such that a 45-degree entry into the downwind leg might crowd another airplane, turn away to the right, in a left-hand pattern, and return for another try. If it's a controlled field, inform the tower; if it's an uncontrolled airport, transmit intentions on the CTAF. If the airport is uncontrolled, you should already have the proper CTAF tuned, because you should have announced your intentions as you approached the field.

CROSSWIND LANDINGS

It seems that almost everyone explains crosswind landings the same way. They tell you that there are two ways to handle such a situation, detail both, and then inform you that one of these methods should not be used. Sort of as an afterthought, most add that a combination of the two methods, the crabbing or "kickout" method, and the wing-low method, is often used.

Employing the crabbing method, you establish the amount of crab necessary to counter the crosswind as you level off from the turn to final approach (FIGS. 4-7 and 4-8). Unless the wind is gusting or there is the possibility of a wind shear, use normal approach airspeed and flaps, unless the owner's manual recommends otherwise. In gusty conditions, increase approach speed by half the amount of the gusts; that is, if you normally approach at 60 knots and the crosswind is 10 knots gusting to 20, increase your approach speed by at least five knots.

Maintaining a ground track by crabbing into the wind is a simple proposition, your crab angle dictated by wind velocity. Use common sense, however, along with the maximum crosswind figure given in the

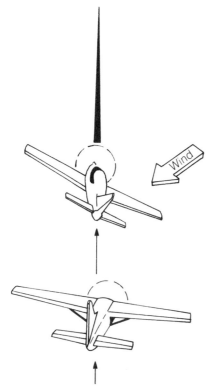

Fig. 4-7. A pilot can crab or slip an aircraft for a crosswind correction.

Fig. 4-8. A crosswind from the right requires a substantial crab angle to keep the aircraft track-
ing down the extended runway centerline on final. The approach is easier this way, but a pilot
cannot afford to land the aircraft in this attitude. An instant before touchdown, the nose must be
yawed straight ahead, quickly and accurately, which is why the wing-low method is usually pre-
ferred.

airplane's owner's manual. While you might be able to maintain your ground track in a strong crosswind, you might not have enough rudder available to "kick out" the crab angle for touchdown, and your landing gear is not designed to land sideways. Many years ago, Goodyear perfected a crosswind landing gear for tailwheel-type airplanes (FIG. 4-9). A pilot maintained the crab right onto the runway, and while the mainwheels castered to roll straight ahead, he sailed down the runway with the airplane pointed at the terminal building. That was an eerie sensation and required a bit of faith.

Carry the crab angle right into the flare with this procedure, and at the last second before the wheels touch, yaw the nose to point straight down the runway. It is not easy because, clearly, you must apply exactly the right amount of rudder. You do not "kick" the rudder pedal any more than you "slam" a control stick forward. Those terms are for fiction stories. If you try this method as a student pilot, what you might feel like

Fig. 4-9. The Goodyear crosswind landing gear for conventional gear aircraft took some getting used to because touchdown and rollout were accomplished while crabbing into the wind.

kicking is your own backside for thinking that you could guess the exact amount of rudder needed at the last instant before touchdown. Either too little rudder or too much rudder is going to result in a side load on the main landing gear. You also need to get the nosewheel down early with this procedure before the airplane has a chance to weathervane as speed dissipates and hold up-aileron into the wind.

The wing-low procedure is the simplest of the two methods and requires no last-second adjustments. Control the airspeed with pitch as usual, and the rate of descent with power, and you will soon become comfortable with this technique. Drop a wing into the wind as you complete the turn from base to final approach; certain pilots initially crab into the wind in order to determine the amount of drift, then switch to the wing-low configuration. The amount of bank needed will depend upon wind velocity. Again, be aware of the maximum allowable crosswind component as listed in the owner's manual.

To compensate for the airplane's tendency to turn into the down wing, opposite rudder is applied to maintain the ground track along the extended centerline of the runway. So, you are in a gentle forward slip all the way down final, and you carry this attitude through a normal flare and touchdown. You will touch down on one wheel, and it is important to keep the wing low and maintain a straight track down the runway with whatever rudder it takes to do the job (FIG. 4-10).

Throughout the flare, and into touchdown and the subsequent roll-out, the flight controls are going to become progressively softer, as they always do with diminishing speed, so you will have to apply more and more control pressure to counter the crosswind. Don't relax aileron pressure to help the other main wheel to settle; it will do so rather quickly on its own if you have properly managed the airspeed. Ground friction on the rolling main exerts all the force necessary to bring down the other main.

Fig. 4-10. Landing in a left crosswind. The left-wing-low attitude naturally means the tire of the left main wheel will touchdown first.

By the time both mains are rolling, you might have the aileron and rudder against their stops. To take advantage of the nosewheel for steering, you can ease off a slight amount of back pressure on the yoke to get the nosewheel down a little sooner than usual. But make certain the rudder is neutral when the nosewheel touches down, otherwise you'll find yourself making a high-speed turnoff much earlier than you had planned. Don't use brakes until all wheels are rolling.

The rollout, taxi, and systems shut-down must be regarded as part of the landing. The flight is not over until the airplane is tied down, hangared, locked, or consigned to the care of trustworthy service personnel. Turbocharged engines need a four- or five-minute cool-down after landing (include taxi time) before shutdown. Two or three minutes at idle power with any reciprocating engine is good insurance against sticking valves and hairline cylinder-head cracks. Then, turn off the boost pump, pull the mixture control into "ideal cutoff," and let the propeller come to a complete stop before turning off the ignition. Finally, turn off all electrical equipment and the master switch.

Combined Method. Many pilots feel uncomfortable flying the wing-low method all the way down final with the turn coordinator's ball out of its cage. Therefore, they fly the crab method down final with the nose of the airplane yawed into the wind while tracking the extended runway centerline. Then, when down to about 100 feet above the surface on short final, they go to the wing-low attitude and enter the flare with the nose pointed straight down the runway centerline. Timing the switch from a crab to wing-low and adding opposite rudder is a function of practice. With practice, you can hold the crab down to 20 or 30 feet right into the beginning of the flare. Of course, in gusty conditions it's best to make the switch a little sooner.

During any crosswind rollout, hold full up-aileron on the upwind wing, and neutral or slightly forward pressure on the yoke. If you must taxi downwind when exiting the runway, do so with full down-elevator.

The pilot's operating handbook will have a graph or table that shows the maximum crosswind component. Much of the time you will have some headwind component and some crosswind component. For example, a wind that is 45° off the runway centerline will have a crosswind component of about 2/3 of the wind velocity. The other 1/3 will be a headwind component.

You will note that the maximum crosswind component as given in the owner's manual will be less than 20 knots for almost all lightplanes—usually closer to 15 knots. If you don't fudge on that figure you won't need to get the upwind wing down very far when employing the wing-low technique. The biggest problems are caused by gusty conditions and wet or icy runways. Normally, you can handle the gusts with a little extra airspeed. A wet or icy runway, swept by a strong crosswind, is probably best handled with prayer.

At uncontrolled airports you may have only the shape of the wind sock as a clue to wind velocity, and it is not going to show you the difference between a 17- and 24-knot wind. Most wind socks, depending upon length, will be fully inflated in any wind greater than 15 knots. If you fly a precise pattern, the drift correction toward or away from the runway might be another clue, although you know the wind is not likely to be exactly the same at an altitude 1,000 feet below.

TAILWHEEL LANDINGS

What about the older classic airplanes with the nosewheel under the tail? Are they as tricky to land as the airport lounge lizards claim? Not too many years ago airplanes with tailwheels were said to have *conventional* landing gear and, presumably, you made conventional landings in them. The three-point landing, power at idle as the mains and tailwheel simultaneously touched lightly with the airplane fully stalled, was regarded as the mark of the accomplished pilot.

Actually, it wasn't all that difficult in, say, a three-place Piper Super Cruiser, which had a wing loading under 10 pounds per square foot and a stalling speed of 42 mph fully loaded, operating from a grass field that allowed you to land and take off directly into the wind each time. It got a bit more difficult as speeds and wing loadings increased and paved runways, rather than wind, dictated landing and takeoff direction.

Until the late 1950s almost everyone learned to fly in tailwheel airplanes, and the first Cessna 150, introduced in 1958, was derisively referred to by some of the old hands as having a "training wheel" or "idiot wheel" under its nose. But the tri-gear prevailed because it is easier to land and therefore results in fewer bent airframes.

If all of your flying is in a tri-gear airplane, take a few hours of dual instruction in a tailwheel airplane before soloing it. The center of gravity is behind the main wheels on airplanes with tailwheels, therefore you must be careful to maintain a straight track down the runway on rollout or the tail will tend to swing around toward the front in what is known as a *ground loop*. The usual result is landing gear and prop damage if you leave the runway and, perhaps, a bashed wingtip, although it's possible to go over on your back if you get excited and stomp the brakes (FIG. 4-11).

I've witnessed several ground loops over the years, perhaps the most

Fig. 4-11. When landing a tailwheel-type aircraft, a pilot must track straight down the runway or the tail will tend to swing around toward the front, causing a classical ground loop. The abrupt turn might be followed by an abrupt stop if the pilot reacts by stomping on the brakes.

interesting performed by a Cessna 195 pilot who did a complete 180 on rollout and came to a stop with the tail where the nose should have been. Then there was the would-be lady aero pilot who let a clipped-wing Cub get away from her during rollout. She got on the brakes, and the Cub went hopping off into the grass with its tail pointed skyward about 45° and its prop shooting sparks. The airplane came to rest on its nose.

As mentioned above, you can land a tailwheel airplane three-point in a full stall, or on the main gear, tail high, with or without power. The power *wheel landing* is certainly preferred for crosswinds. For a wheel landing, set up a normal approach at normal approach speed, higher than normal speed in gusty and/or crosswind conditions, and hold the airplane level after your flare, just a couple of feet above the runway. Then, a slight power reduction will allow the airplane to settle onto its mains. At this point, go forward slightly on the stick, or yoke, to keep the tail up and prevent the airplane from ballooning back into the air. Don't worry about the prop striking the runway; at touchdown velocity you probably could not force the tail that high with the wheels rolling.

If the wheel landing is made power-off, do it the same way except, instead of reducing power for touchdown, relax back pressure on the stick a little to let the airplane settle onto the mains and, again, ease in some forward stick to hold the airplane in level attitude until speed dissipates.

When a tailwheel airplane is in a three-point attitude, tail down, the wing tends to cancel some of the airflow over the tail (FIG. 4-12). The situation is compounded during a full-stall landing with power at idle and the resulting weak slipstream. Some rudder is desirable to help the tailwheel keep the rollout straight ahead. Three-point an old biplane that

Fig. 4-12. A three-point, full-stall landing is easier if the wind cooperates. Any pilot who learned to fly in a tricycle gear aircraft should go to the expense of dual instruction from an experienced tailwheel airplane instructor before flying a conventional gear aircraft.

has a tailskid in place of a steerable tailwheel, and you will appreciate the rudder.

The three-point landing in a taildragger has long been described as stalling the airplane about six inches above the surface, power at idle. The flare is managed so that the stick is back against the stops as the airplane settles on mains and tailwheel simultaneously. No points are subtracted if the tailwheel touches slightly before the main wheels, but if the main gear is solidly down while the tail is still flying, it's probably best to treat it as a power-off wheel landing and complete the landing accordingly.

So what is the secret of consistently good tailwheel landings? The key is to hold the tail on the ground during rollout and make prompt corrections to maintain a straight track. A good tailwheel installation, with strong springs and a horizontally mounted swivel plate, is extremely important. Also, taxi these airplanes at a leisurely pace with a series of S-turns providing good forward vision.

Brakes are important on a tailwheel airplane because they are sometimes needed to augment the action of the steerable tailwheel in a crosswind, and because they can become your only means of steering on rollout if the tailwheel shimmies and becomes ineffective due to weak springs, bent control arms, or excessive wear. Don't be heavy-footed and lock-up the downwind brake; tap the brakes lightly, then increase pressure as needed.

WET AND ICY

Hydroplaning, the development of a film of water between tires and the runway surface, can begin at 38−40 knots in lightplanes, depending upon aircraft weight and tire pressure. The type of surface is also a factor. Asphalt, of course, is highly conducive to this condition while grooved concrete is not. Hydroplaning is a dangerous situation because you lack both control and braking efficiency.

When faced with a wet runway, that is, wet enough that hydroplaning might be a factor, your landing technique will be dictated by wind conditions. At controlled airports, the ATIS broadcast will include braking action advisories, and Tower will give them, too. If the wind is no more than 10° off the runway, you haven't too much of a problem, even in a tailwheel airplane. But keep in mind that even this depends upon wind velocity, because the headwind you land into becomes a crosswind as you taxi off the runway, and it might be too strong to taxi on a slick surface.

A crosswind landing on a slick surface can be a challenge in a tri-gear and an adventure in a tailwheel airplane and your options are limited.

Fig. 4-13. Skis require special techniques and new rules. Dual training from an experienced instructor would be a very wise decision before flying an aircraft with skis.

In a tri-gear airplane you can limit yourself to a maximum crosswind component of 50 percent or normal and employ short-field landing techniques, or you can insist upon landing into the wind, especially if you are flying a tailwheel airplane. The latter choice could mean going to another airport or landing in the grass. Some airports with paved runways also have designated grass strips. If the airport is controlled, ask the controller. It's true that wet grass doesn't offer much in the way of a good braking surface, but it is still an option if you need to eliminate an unacceptable crosswind. It requires soft-field technique which is discussed in the next chapter.

Ice and packed snow on the runway constitute the worst landing situations with any significant crosswind, along with the fewest options (FIG. 4-13). Common sense will be your principal guide, which means that, if employed soon enough, you leave the airplane in the hangar. Most of us have had experience driving our automobiles on ice, and it appears that many of our fellow drivers tend to lose all reason once the drive wheels lose traction. On perfectly level streets they can be seen spinning their wheels at high speed, tires smoking, as they floorboard the accelerator pedal and go nowhere. Meanwhile, drivers with a modicum of self-discipline and common sense, barely touching their accelerators, move gingerly around the wheel-spinners and proceed to their destinations.

The wheels of an airplane have no power. If you must use an icy runway, short-field technique is probably best if the surface is smooth; soft-field technique if the wind has carved humps and ridges. Stay off the brakes.

You can't always judge the condition of a runway by observing it from the air, and the presence of a control tower or flight service station is no guarantee that you will be informed of all possible undesirable situations. I remember going into controlled Wiley Post Airport at Bethany, Oklahoma, one winter morning when I could see pretty white patterns across the runway that looked like ripples on a pond. I assumed that it was wind-blown snow. It wasn't. It was wind-blown *sleet* that had frozen solid in little ridges three or four inches high. I don't know why that ice didn't wipe out the Comanche's nose gear or blow a tire or two. That was a rough rollout.

Crosswind landings are certainly interesting on icy runways, and included in the standard advice for handling such situations is the suggestion that you land on the upwind edge of the runway and trust that you can complete a rollout before drifting off the downwind edge of the runway or weathervaning and sliding sideways into a snow bank. Fly the standard crosswind approach, and touch down on the upwind main. The other main might need a tiny bit of help due to reduced surface friction. Then get the nosewheel down. Do not use brakes and because you are using no more than 20 percent of flaps, just leave them as is. Flap retraction is not going to help much in transferring weight to the wheels more quickly and you don't need another distraction at this point. Use your flight controls to the fullest, because that is all you have, and expect the rudder to become ineffective below about $30-35$ knots.

If you find the above advice inadequate compared to what you had hoped for, then I suggest that you face up to the truth with me: There are some things that you should not try in an airplane until you have years of flying experience. By that time, you will know better than to try them.

A cleared runway with icy patches is another situation that calls for no brakes. The danger of asymmetrical braking, which would spin the airplane into a sudden ground loop, overrides any benefit you might derive from the use of brakes.

Visibility, or the lack of it, might dictate landing techniques akin to those sometimes employed at night, which is covered in the next chapter. Visibility in cold weather can be fabulous away from industrial areas, but there are also those dark and hazy days when recent snowfall makes depth perception difficult, particularly at small uncontrolled airports. Here you can borrow from the floatplane pilot's textbook: Set up a 100–150 fpm rate of descent on final approach and hold it right into touchdown. There is no law that says you have to flare in the ground cushion—airliners never do.

If you are forced to land in mud, slush, snow, or a combination of these, it's best to extend no more than 20–25° of flaps and carry a little extra airspeed onto the runway with the nose high. The drag of the mushy surface on the landing gear will tend to pitch the nose down, and meanwhile the extra airspeed will help keep the flight controls effective until a straight rollout is established. Land a tailwheel airplane the same way on such a surface.

TAXIWAY LANDINGS

Shivers run down the spine of any safety-minded pilot when he thinks about landing with a strong crosswind. Those shivers might be beneficial and actually make the pilot more aware of correct procedures to control the aircraft and land safely. Many pilots simply refuse to fly on a windy crosswind day, which is probably wise because if the pilot has few hours and is uncomfortable with crosswinds, then avoidance when possible is a correct decision.

Sometimes avoidance is impossible. Certainly, if a pilot wants to fly locally for an hour or two, the weather is likely going to hold. Avoidance is not an option when a pilot encounters unforecast winds at a destination airport at the conclusion of a long cross-country flight. Ideally, a pilot should stay up-to-date regarding the destination weather by contacting flight watch en route and requesting weather at the destination, if weather observations are made, or in the area surrounding the destination. Monitoring ATIS at, or in the vicinity of, a destination might inform the pilot soon enough to select an alternate airport with an appropriate runway for the prevailing winds.

Realistically, the first time that a pilot might realize that an ill-wind is blowing would be upon spotting the wind sock, tee, or tetrahedron when approaching the airport. It is frightening to cross over an airport's single north-south runway—above the pattern altitude—and see a wind sock pointing straight out and straight east. One student pilot had never seen a direct crosswind until reaching his destination of the required 100-mile solo cross-country. He had to land to get the logbook endorsement and make a personal pit stop, not necessarily in that order.

The early portion of the final approach was a bobbing and weaving adventure that seemed to beg for a go-around. But the student pilot stabilized the aircraft and continued the approach. A combination of crabbing and cross-controlling worked well enough that the pilot put the aircraft down safely, although too fast (most of the runway was required to shed the excess speed), then he doublebacked down the runway, and safely exited for taxi to the airfield's FSS.

Takeoff proved less adventurous, but moments after exiting the traffic pattern, the student pilot realized that he had not made the personal pit stop; choppy turbulence made for a wild and desperate ride home where another direct crosswind was waiting. The aircraft proved difficult to control upon landing, and the experience proved to be a valuable lesson.

Ten years later the by-now certified pilot was faced with a 25-knot, right-quartering crosswind at the conclusion of a comparatively short 1.5-hour cross-country, but at the end of a very hectic workweek. He was tired and was flying with less than ideal efficiency, but with proper judgment. Fortunately, this uncontrolled airport was the pilot's home field and he knew the lay of the land. Also fortunately, a wind that strong at such an angle to the main runway grounded any fun flyers that day; therefore, the pilot had the run of the place, which he verified by monitoring unicom, requesting a traffic advisory from unicom, and scanning.

Two runways at the airport intersected near the end of each runway. A diagonal taxiway connected the opposite end of one runway to approximately three-quarters of the way down to the opposite end of the other runway, forming a right-angle triangle. That was the key. The diagonal taxiway was straight into the wind. The pilot flew the aircraft over the airport slightly below pattern altitude at a less-than-normal cruise airspeed. The tetrahedron pointed directly parallel to the taxiway, and the wind sock was steady: direct taxiway headwind, no noticeable gusts.

No traffic was in the area. The pilot announced on the unicom his intentions to land on the taxiway—at that time unicom did not carry a CTAF designator—and flew a traffic pattern that avoided the surrounding neighborhoods without jeopardizing the precision necessary to make the landing. Each heading change and power reduction was a benchmark for the pilot to consider executing a go-around; under the circumstances, this would not be a must-land approach.

Everything went well, even crossing over imaginary numbers at a proper altitude, starting to flair. Then a problem arose when the taxiway unexpectedly started to slope downhill away from the aircraft. A quick glance beyond the unexpected sloping revealed a rise in the taxiway; he held the flair, the aircraft sank a few more feet, then the taxiway rose gradually to meet the main gear in what proved to be a very smooth landing.

Plenty of taxiway remained, but the pilot was able to stop the aircraft, turn around and taxi the aircraft to the fuel pump. He subsequently learned that other pilots had used the taxiway under similar conditions, and apparently low-level patrol pilots had been known to use the airport's expansive tarmac for extremely short landings to avoid strong crosswinds.

Lessons Learned

A few years later the same pilot could have applied the lessons learned as a student and a certificated flyer to avoid a less than wonderful landing. The saving grace was that he landed the aircraft without his passenger knowing what had happened. This time, a left-quartering crosswind faced the aircraft and pilot. Crabbing held the aircraft straight down the centerline until crossing the proverbial, and actual, fence. Cross-controlling during the final approach had prepared the pilot for the necessity of making heading adjustments during the flair. Unfortunately, the aircraft was hot, sank a bit faster than expected, and bounced mightily. Two more bounces were required to get down safely. Not pretty, but successful.

Later that night, resting comfortably in bed, the pilot recalled that this airport also had a taxiway that might have been safe for landing into a more direct headwind. But he did not know the exact lay of the land around this airport, and the presence of a passenger tempered any regrets that he did not land on the taxiway of this uncontrolled airport. This instance proved that dealing primarily with the wind and an established runway is a better option when passengers must be considered. Insurance considerations must arise in every instance; potentially, in the event of and accident, an insurance company would probably frown on any deviations from recognizably safe operations.

Taxiway Landing Canceled

Another pilot would have landed on the taxiway at a tower-controlled airport if the airport had not gone below minimums. The runway was partially obscured by blowing dust, but a localizer approach brought the pilot to within sight of the approach lights that lead to the end of the runway. A taxiway angled into a run-up area at the end of that runway; the taxiway faced directly into the crosswind.

Somewhere between the outer marker and the middle marker, just as the runway and taxiway came into sight, the tower controller announced that the visibility had worsened to below conditions and a landing on the runway would be required. (The instrument-rated pilot was already on an instrument flight plan, which he picked up from the approach control facility. If the pilot had not been instrument-rated, he could have requested a special VFR clearance for landing.)

The pilot balked to himself and whimsically asked the controller, presumably to break the tension and loosen up, what it would take to land on the taxiway. ATC replied that declaring an emergency would do the trick; the pilot subsequently requested clearance for landing on the main runway. A noticeable crab into the wind continued until the last moment, when the pilot straightened the aircraft, which simultaneously stalled and touched down on the main landing gear.

5
Short, Soft, and Dark

THE FLIGHT PORTION OF THE PRIVATE PILOT EXAMINATION REQUIRES that you demonstrate both short- and soft-field landing techniques. Both are rather easily mastered. The hard part is staying in practice when you have become proficient at them. Many pilots promptly forget these procedures soon after the flight examiner steps from the airplane. They have never operated from less than a mile of concrete, and they tend to view short-field and soft-field landings as training exercises, like ground reference maneuvers. That attitude usually doesn't last.

SHORT-FIELD APPROACH AND LANDING

One thing should be said in the beginning about short- and soft-field landings. The fact that you do not intend to use a lot of ground does not necessarily mean that you should fly a tight pattern with an abbreviated final approach. Just the opposite is true, wind and surrounding terrain permitting. When possible, take your time, fly a standard pattern, and give yourself plenty of room on final to set things up as carefully as you can. Extend full flaps as soon as you level out on final approach, and get the airspeed stabilized at no more than 1.3 V_{so}, assuming that you are not also faced with turbulence or gusty wind conditions.

Getting full flaps down early, perhaps before you are certain that you have the field made, is contrary to your usual procedure, but you might be a little higher than normal to clear obstructions just off the runway threshold, and early deployment of full flaps allows more time to stabilize the approach so that the only control change you should need is a touch of power.

If you are too high, do not dive for the runway. Reduce power if you can; otherwise, apply full power and go around for another try.

I once heard short-field landings described as being "like any other landings, except more so." That is a good description. It is important that you select the desired touchdown spot and stick with it. The short-field landing is a precision landing. In actual practice, a number of factors must be taken into account when planning any landing, but *real* short-field landings often include wind conditions and topography that are normally seldom confronted.

Wind is always a factor and can be tricky in mountain country. Temperature is important, and heat combined with high altitude means a high *true* airspeed (TAS), although the *indicated* airspeed (IAS) is right where it should be. Where should it be? The operating handbook might give a lower figure, which is all right in smooth air and no possibility of terrain-induced turbulence, but the regular approach speed of 1.3 times flaps-down power-off stall speed is usually a safe figure for the approach. The indicated airspeed is the one you use, of course, because it is the one the airplane *feels*. At any given weight and attitude the plane will always stall at the same IAS regardless of the TAS. If you have trouble picturing the relationship between IAS (where the needle points on the airspeed indicator) and TAS, remember that the airspeed indicator is a pressure instrument; you have to go faster through thin air to make it indicate the same as it would going slower in denser air.

The spot you select for touchdown must allow a safe margin over any obstacles on the approach and provide the maximum possible rollout area beyond touchdown. It's best to make this approach under power and with a higher-than-usual angle of attack, using pitch to control airspeed. Cut power just before touchdown, and apply brakes as soon as the mains are rolling. Brake smoothly, with increasing pressure; don't stomp the brakes. Keep the yoke all the way back—ideally it should reach the stops just as the mains touch—and retract the flaps as soon as you can to get the weight on the main wheels and increase brake effectiveness.

There is another way to do it, usually referred to as "dragging it in," which gets the airspeed way down, actually below the airplane's normal power-off stall speed. The approach is flown with a high power setting and very high angle of attack. You are literally "hanging on the prop," and when the throttle is cut, the airplane quits flying immediately. This is actually an emergency procedure that requires a fine touch; but later, as you gain experience, you should know how to do it in your airplane just in case it ever becomes necessary.

I once saw Larry Ball demonstrate this procedure in a 260-hp Bonanza V-tail. At the time, Larry was in charge of Bonanza sales at the Beech factory, and I had gone to Wichita for a demo ride. Not many people have more time in V-tails than Larry. He had a new airplane and a cool day, and we were 200 pounds under gross. Still, it was an impressive demonstration.

The two of us flew over to Newton, Kansas, for what Larry characterized as "minimum-field" landings. That's flat country, and there were no obstacles to a low approach. With gear and flaps down, nose high, and under high power, Ball made the approach at 50 mph IAS, which was 10 mph below the gear-and-flaps-down-power-off stalling speed listed in the owner's manual. As the runway threshold disappeared under our nose, Larry closed the throttle, the Bonanza was on the pavement immediately, and we stopped in approximately 330 feet. I was able to obtain a fairly close measurement because I left the airplane and determined that the expansion joints in the runway were 21 feet apart. The wind was on our nose at 5 to 10 mph. I don't recall the temperature or altimeter setting, but it was a nice demonstration, I thought, and I included it in a little book I did about those airplanes. However, it turned out that Larry thought we were just stooging around and did not understand that I intended to write about the events of that morning. When he saw it in print, he asked that we add 10 mph to his approach speed because, he said, an inexperienced pilot, trying to duplicate the procedure in a Bonanza, might get into trouble. After so many years, maybe Larry will forgive me if I tell it like it really was.

SOFT-FIELD LANDINGS

The *soft-field landing* is accomplished by what I choose to describe as a "modified drag-in." Use approximately 50 percent power during approach, with full flaps and gear down, maintaining an IAS of 1.3 V_{so} or a little less, and controlling airspeed with pitch as usual. This should allow some flexibility in the descent rate because you can add or subtract a little power as required and achieve good precision in touching down quite close beyond your reference spot.

Fig. 5-1. A Stationair flairs during a soft-field landing with a proper power setting and proper airspeed for the pilot to control the aircraft.

Now, pay attention; here's how to touch like a feather (FIG. 5-1). As you descend to the height where you normally begin your flare, continue back pressure on the yoke to further erode your airspeed, and slowly increase power. Now, you are working on the back side of your power curve (some call it the "area of reverse command"), with airspeed below V_{so}, and as long as you continue to apply up-elevator, that additional power is going to result in slower flight.

All of your attention must be outside the airplane. Keep the airplane straight with rudder and allow no side drift. If this is an off-airport landing, try to select a prominent terrain feature in the distance to use as a straight-ahead guide. You do these last few feet by feel alone. The IAS will be without value anyway, because you are at least five knots below your normal touchdown speed.

With the nose high and under power, you will very gradually descend to the surface. With a little practice, your wheels will touch ever so lightly. As soon as you are sure you have touched down, you may cut power to the extent desired. Usually, surface conditions and wind will make this decision for you. In soft ground or snow, you might want to keep moving and taxi to a firmer surface. Keep the nosewheel light with up-elevator, and don't use brakes except in an emergency. Many instructors will tell you to get the flaps up to avoid damaging them with rocks, ice, etc. (FIG. 5-2). But if the surface is really soft and the situation argues that you keep moving, it has always seemed to me that it's better to

Fig. 5-2. An old asphalt runway in the high desert is treated as a soft field because it contains soft spots. Ask pilots who fly in the area about the condition of primitive landing strips in the West and Southwest.

keep the airplane as light on its wheels as possible by taking whatever tiny amount of lift you can get at that speed. A fast taxi is not a good idea on a soft surface. If the main wheels are momentarily slowed by any kind of obstacle, that can cause the nosewheel to burrow into the mush. The pace of a brisk walk is the best taxi speed. The important thing is to keep moving.

As I noted earlier, there are people around who have not practiced short- or soft-field landings since certified, but I am privileged to know some very good pilots who seldom land any other way. They do short-field landings on 8,600-foot runways in the flatlands. They clearly put a lot of effort into each landing. It's not just pride, though I'm sure there is some of that involved, but also the fact that it keeps their skills sharply honed for those occasions when such techniques are essential.

GRASS AIRSTRIPS

Study any sectional chart, especially those covering areas outside the Northeast air corridor, and you might be surprised at the number of unpaved airport symbols you can find. There might be more places you can land a lightplane on grass than on concrete or asphalt.

If you plan to fly into a grass strip that is strange to you, phone ahead to determine field condition, along with anything else the operator or FBO can tell you, *including how to locate it from the air*. If the field is unattended, use extreme caution. A hard rain within the past 48 hours might have left the field too soft for safe operation, although this depends upon the type of soil and drainage, and the amount of sun and wind since the rain. Another problem is that some grass strips in the boonies may remain on sectionals when they are no longer maintained as landing areas.

The barnstormers of the 1920s used strange grass fields almost exclusively. One such barnstormer, the late Earl Reed, who obtained the first clipped-wing Cub STC, told me that standard procedure was to inspect the pasture selected for operations (it had to be on the edge of town and bordering a road) by making a couple of slow passes at 100 feet to look for obstacles such as gopher holes, rocks, and deep ruts caused by ground vehicles. They also looked for hog feeding troughs not in use, which worked well as wheel chocks. It's unlikely that you will find a handy hog trough, but the rest of Earl's procedure remains valid. Get down low and slow and inspect the unattended field as best you can if you absolutely must land there. In my view, it's better to fly a little farther, land where conditions are known, and make up the difference in rented wheels.

Operating from a grass airport, whether your home field or a strange one, your concerns are what common sense tells you they should be: Is the ground soft from recent rain or thaw? Does the grass hide ruts, holes, rocks, or other obstacles? Are there high tension wires bordering the field, and are they marked with orange balls? Is there a phone?

As for flight operations, use soft-field technique. Taxi slowly, and don't expect good braking in wet grass. If you are flying a tri-gear airplane, hold the nose off as long as you can when landing, and take off tail-low, the idea being to give your nosewheel every break you can. Grass, depending upon its height, can add up to 50 percent to a normal takeoff roll. Therefore, it is sometimes desirable to help the airplane fly off at minimum airspeed and then hold it level in ground effect until you have accelerated to your climb speed, best rate, V_y, or best angle, V_x, as the environment dictates.

If you regularly operate from a grass field, check the air intake filter often, and include a careful inspection of the wheel brake assemblies in each preflight inspection. Keep them free of mud and debris. Tailwheel assemblies also gather a lot of weeds and mud. Pilots who are based on grass fields sometimes re-route hydraulic brake lines to the rear edges of exposed gear legs. They also tape the leading edge of the horizontal stabilizer.

IN THE MOUNTAINS

In the western United States there are many airports above 5,000 feet elevation. A few are major terminals; most serve smaller communities. In the mountains, runways are sometimes short and occasionally unpaved, the winds seemingly unpredictable. Surface winds in the mountains are seldom steady, which means higher landing speeds to compensate for gusts. The increased airspeed, plus increased ground speed, due to the thinner air and higher density altitude, translate into significantly higher touchdown speeds.

Most airports in the high country are located so that you can, and are expected to, fly a normal traffic pattern. At uncontrolled fields, announce your position and intentions on the published CTAF frequency five miles out and again just prior to each turn in the pattern. Make every effort to determine surface wind conditions, overflying the strip above pattern altitude, if necessary. Lacking a response from unicom, you'll have to use an altimeter setting from the nearest flight service station (FSS).

The surrounding terrain might dictate that you fly the final approach a bit high, and in gusty conditions the best approach speed should typically be the same as the best rate-of-climb speed, with $20-25°$ of flaps deployed. If you have to abort the landing and go around for another approach, you will appreciate the extra airspeed and the fact that you are not carrying full flaps, but the prime reason for this configuration is to have adequate control through the touchdown and rollout.

Retract flaps immediately after touchdown. On hard surfaces with uncooperative winds, get the nosewheel down early. Be aware that, with high density altitude the flare prior to touchdown will not check the rate of descent as it does in denser air, and be prepared to soften the landing with a touch of power.

It is important to determine which way, if any, the airstrip slopes. Uphill runways can trick you into believing that you are higher than you are, while a landing area or runway that slopes downhill can make you think you are lower than you actually are. Sloping runways also do not allow the use of a fixed reference with which to judge the touchdown point.

Except for the capricious winds and the lack of weathercasts, the greatest concern for the average lightplane pilot in mountain flying is dealing with the question of density altitude. You will recall from ground school classes that *pressure altitude* is your indicated altitude with the altimeter set at 29.92 Hg. Corrected for temperature, it is density altitude, which is the altitude at which the airplane thinks it is operating, regardless of its actual height above either sea level or the terrain below.

The density altitude of an airport located at 5,000 feet elevation can easily be 6,000 feet or more at noon on a warm day, higher if a low pressure air mass covers the area. If you refer to the takeoff chart in the airplane's owner's manual, you will note that you start with a gross weight and find the required takeoff run and the distance for a takeoff over a 50-foot obstacle after including wind, altitude, and temperature. There might be a small fudge factor included, but I think it's wise to add another 5 − 10 percent for aircraft age and less-than-perfect pilot technique.

In mountain country, dependable weathercasts are rare. Weather reporting stations are spread thinly over the western states, and mountains make their own mini-weather systems. Light zephyrs squeezing through mountain passes from the west can come roaring out the eastern side at 50 knots. Orographic thunderstorms develop when a relatively moist air mass, usually off the Pacific, is pushed up the western slopes of the mountains by the prevailing westerlies until it reaches its dew point. Convective thunderstorms also form over the mountains on summer afternoons.

In the valleys, the mountains' leeward slopes are generally to be avoided. The wind spilling over the summit rolls down toward the valley floor, affected by terrain irregularities. Surface friction tends to slow the air mass, but it also causes turbulence.

Wind shear is common in the mountains and can occur vertically as well as horizontally. It can be the result of a *microburst* from the bottom of a mature thunderhead or other convective activity, or it can be caused by a warm air mass flowing across a mass of cooler air trapped in a valley. There is surprisingly little mixing together of two dissimilar air masses when they come together, and there will always be a turbulent transition zone along the boundaries.

NIGHT LANDINGS

Sometimes, walking through the pilots' lounge, you can hear some interesting statements: "If you go flying at night in a single-engine airplane, you start out with an emergency." But you know how pilots are. They either overstate or understate to get a point across. Lots of people routinely fly single-engine airplanes on night cross-countries and think nothing of it.

I know one pilot who flies his Cessna Cardinal on night cross-countries between lighted airports that are no more than 30 miles apart. He reasons that, in the event of engine failure, from a cruising altitude of at least 10,000 feet he can almost certainly glide 15 miles to the nearest landing patch. I suppose that works all right in the eastern part of the United States, but west of the Mississippi, airports are fewer and farther between. There, some of us tend to follow the interstates at low altitudes, secure in the belief that we have an emergency landing strip just below throughout the flight. The rest of us seek no painless sops to our fears, believing that the best insurance against a forced landing is good preflight planning and a properly maintained airplane, along with the judgment to fly or not to fly based upon the capability of our airplanes and ourselves for each situation.

I regard the light twins, 180 horsepower on each side, with 4,000-foot single-engine ceilings as far more risky at night than a single-engine airplane, which has a single-engine service ceiling three times higher. That 4,000-foot ceiling soon dwindles to zero over the Alleghenies or west of Amarillo. Over more than half of the country there's no margin for a hot summer night or a little dab of ice on the wings.

Admittedly, that's no way to justify a decision to fly single-engine at night. You do it because you weigh the risk against the need and then hold your thumb on the faith side of the scale. It's a personal decision.

Approaching controlled airports at night, you will be told when and how to enter the traffic pattern. At uncontrolled fields, always fly a standard pattern, transmitting your position and intentions on the appropriate CTAF. Because it is often difficult to judge height above the surface as you near the runway, an accurate altimeter setting is important, and you need to know airport elevation, along with direction and velocity. It's often difficult enough to find a wind indicator on a strange airport in daytime, but at night it can be even worse. You might have to overfly the field looking for it.

Some instructors advise flying a steep approach at night, but it seems to me that a normal approach, carrying enough power so that you have the flexibility to shorten or lengthen the final as necessary, is the surest way. Use 20–25° of flaps.

If you should find yourself following an airliner on final approach, plan your touchdown at least halfway down the runway in order to avoid its dangerous wake turbulence. At night, you'll find it very difficult to tell just where the big jet actually touches down, which is where those twin tornadoes spiraling off his wingtips cease. You can usually assume that he will be on the concrete before using up half of it. The remaining half should be plenty for you.

In all cases, maintain the proper spacing between your airplane and the one ahead, particularly if it is a big one. The controller is supposed to do this and is supposed to do it with regard to wake turbulence, but some towers are closed during the wee hours, although airline and military traffic might continue.

The problem with night landings is that of judging distance, or depth perception. Your eyes' depth perceptor works just as well at night, but the clues it gets are too few and too inconsistent too often. For example, because a runway can have any width, the distance between the left and right rows of runway lights is not standard. A night landing at an unfamiliar airport can therefore be interesting, even on the clearest of nights. You can look straight down the runway from short final and be thoroughly confused. Wide spacing between the rows of lights can give you the impression that you are higher than normal, while rows that are closer together than you have been accustomed to can give you the impression that you are low. VASIs have aided a great deal in this respect, especially if you have resisted the temptation to habitually expand on their directions. Approach light systems can also help give you some perspective of runway dimensions.

I won't try to explain all of that rod and cone business about the human eyeball because I don't remember much of it and doubt if you care that much anyway. It's probably enough to say that you have a blind spot in the focal center of your eye at night that covers about $5°$, and that is why your vision improves when you direct your eyes $10°$ or so from the object to be seen.

Stare vision is one of the tricks your eyes can play at night, when a fixed or stationary light appears to move in wide arcs. If the light is moving, it might seem to move to one side while in reality it is moving straight ahead. So, don't stare; keep shifting from one point to another.

One of the most significant results of an Air Force study of night vision problems was that people who normally spend from two to five hours in bright sunshine in the afternoon require up to five hours to adapt to darkness. That is why you should wear sunglasses. Air Force specifications are for sunglasses that admit no more than 15 percent of bright sunlight. A specialist in pilot's visual problems, optometrist Warren DeHaan of Boulder, Colorado, who holds an airline transport pilot certificate, recommends lenses of reddish-brown or gray tint.

Night flight has its compensations. The air is generally smoother, controllers aren't as busy, and because strobe lights have become common on airplanes, other aircraft are much easier to see—that is, if they are at your level or above. Airplanes below and over a city, where they might be approaching the same uncontrolled airport you intend as a destination, tend to blend into the mass of lights below.

When the runway is made, reduce power, continue down, and begin the flare at what you perceive to be approximately a wingspan above the surface. As you flare, bring in enough power to hold the airplane in landing attitude above the runway. Then, a slight power reduction will allow the airplane to gently settle until the main wheels begin to roll: soft-field technique.

Once on the ground at a strange airport, there is often a bewildering array of lights in all directions to intimidate you. The controller will always direct you off the runway onto a blue-lighted taxiway, but if he is busy he might appear to lose interest in you at that point. At large airports, he will hand you over to Ground Control, and that controller will direct you to wherever you want to go on the airport. If you don't receive these directions, ask for them, using the radio frequency of your last contact. Do not switch from tower frequency until told to do so.

After your turn off onto a taxiway, keep the landing, or taxi, light on. There is no telling what you might encounter on a taxiway.

It must be recognized that there is more than one kind of night flight. There is the kind that you can fly soon after sunset, just before sunrise, on one of those clear nights will a full moon, and on nice evenings when the profusion of surface lights provide a definite horizon and other visual references. You can limit night flying to such conditions and log the required landings to satisfy the currency provisions of your pilot's certificate. But that kind of night flying does not prepare you for cross-country VFR for any appreciable distance. Sometimes, it can get pretty dark out there.

One night not long ago, a pilot and his wife died. He was an automobile dealer from a town in northern Oklahoma. He and his wife had spent the evening with friends, then took off to fly home shortly before midnight. He filed special VFR because of a thin layer of fog that had begun to form during the previous hour. As he took off, he almost immediately began a climbing turn to the left and continued around a great arc until impact a mile from the airport.

About a year later, I lost a longtime friend in an almost identical situation, except that he took off shortly before sunrise and filed no flight plan. There was a light fog, later reported as $1/16$ mile. He was airborne about two minutes. Three companions died with him.

Both of these tragedies could have easily been avoided. All these pilots had to do (short of delaying takeoff) was set their directional gyros to conform with the runway heading prior to takeoff and then hold that heading during climbout.

This brings up the proposition that a growing number of pilots are endorsing: All night cross-country should be IFR. I have come to support this position despite my proclivity to resist any federal regulation that isn't absolutely necessary to the sun coming up tomorrow. However, I can tell you that you aren't likely to fly night cross-country VFR for very long before you find yourself in IFR conditions. It's a little unsettling to be sailing along on a clear night, all the needles obedient to your wishes, and suddenly note a rosy glow around your wingtip as your navigation light reflects the presence of cloud.

In fact, you can become totally disoriented at night when there is no impediment to visibility. I remember such an occasion. The late Chuck Wolfe and I left Mercedes, Texas, which is way down at the southern tip of Texas on the Mexican border, in a Bellanca Viking about 9 p.m. and climbed into a moonless but unlimited sky that was absolutely crowded with stars. I've never been on the ground down there, but I'm sure there is nothing but sandhills and coyotes, maybe a ranch house here and there. On a moonless night, from 9,500 feet the surface is solid black, punctuated by an occasional, tiny light.

As we progressed toward San Antonio, I found it increasingly difficult to tell where the horizon should be. Then I had the feeling that we were climbing steeply. I could not distinguish between the stars and the lights on the ground. The attitude gyro showed straight and level. I looked at Wolfe in the dim light of the instruments and saw that he was looking at me. I'm sure that he read the situation perfectly (he was an old Navy pilot). He motioned to the glow of a city in the distance of the right wing. "We can get some great seafood over at Corpus Christi," he said.

I banked toward the patch of light, concentrating on the attitude indicator. "You want to take it?" I asked/suggested.

I felt slightly dizzy, and I was angry with myself. I should have filed IFR. I should have gone on autopilot. I should have had more sense.

Wolfe dialed in the new heading and engaged the autopilot. The seafood was indeed great.

My point is that vertigo is an insidious thing. It can happen to anyone under a variety of conditions, even on a perfectly clear night.

One other observation about night flight from personal experience: My night vision improved dramatically after I stopped smoking. I hate to agree with all those meddling do-gooders who make such an issue of it, but I've got to tell it like it is.

No Lights at night

A low-time private pilot without a night flying endorsement was faced with flying at night on a regular basis for business reasons. Two night flights with an instructor were scheduled to obtain the endorsement. The pilot thought it would be a straightforward process and looked forward to concurrently obtaining the biennial flight review endorsement. But he did more than merely shoot a few touch-and-gos and log time cruising around at night. The wise instructor took the time to actually instruct the pilot about safe night operations.

A flashlight was the first order of business. The pilot would soon learn that two flashlights were better: for well-lit preflight checks, a large one that used three D-cell batteries and for cabin illumination, a small one that used AA penlight batteries. The instructor subsequently suggested taping a white opaque piece of plastic over the smaller flashlight to diffuse the light and create a nonglaring, but still bright, glow for panel illumination.

The pilot had flown several times at night in the right seat of a Twin Comanche, so the initial thrill of flying at night was a bit worn, but the thrill of doing the flying was incomparable to merely riding along. The instructor could not emphasize enough how important it was to ensure a climb after takeoff. Simple enough, no positive climb rate meant no cushion was established. Therefore, the vertical speed indicator became an essential instrument for night flying. Airwork consisted of steep turns, stalls, tracking a VOR, and the like. The artificial horizon became an extremely important part of the scan to verify wings level and, again upon takeoff, to verify nose-up for climbing. A new scanning element was maintaining a sense for the horizon and the ground and watching for the unexpected. Primarily, the instructor said, watch for inconsistent patterns in the stars and in the ground lights because any darkened areas might be clouds that should be avoided at all costs.

Altitude Is Insurance

At the instructor's request to land at a nearby airport, the night student immediately reduced power to initiate a descent. The instructor calmly reapplied the power and asked the pilot to fly to the airport at cruise altitude. The instructor explained that altitude was insurance at night and that unnecessarily descending at night might prove unwise if the engine faltered or failed. Upon reaching the airport, at approximately 4,000 feet agl, the instructor pulled the power and applied carburetor heat, then told the pilot to glide in a counterclockwise circle above the airport to keep the runway in sight at all times. Wind direction would be determined and runway selection made in time to fly a compact traffic pattern to final approach, still high enough to S-turn or slip to the runway for landing. Landing long would be acceptable.

The first lesson ended with several normal touch-and-gos at the familiar home airport. The second lesson started where the first lesson ended—with pattern work. However, this time, after the pilot had proven a mastery of takeoff and landing, the instructor switched off the landing light and the cockpit lights during the base leg. A camping trick of holding the small flashlight in the mouth illuminated the instrument panel, leaving both hands free to fly the aircraft.

"Trust the runway lights for a general reference," the instructor said, "but remember they set up off the ground." A sea of black surrounded by two straight rows of lights faced the pilot. "Flare as usual over the numbers, then focus on the runway end lights, maintaining the space from the lights to the top of the cowling while the aircraft settles in and lands," the instructor said.

After a few more touch-and-gos, they departed for a practice area to practice hoodwork and the standard unusual attitude recoveries. Within the next two years, the private pilot flew more often at night than during the day. And more often than not the pilot would not turn off the landing light during short final to maintain proficiency. (The landing light was illuminated whenever the aircraft was operating in the vicinity of an airport at night. The pilot subsequently adopted a safety practice of always illuminating the landing light, day or night, in the vicinity of an airport.)

6
Emergency Landings

MANY OF TODAY'S CIVILIAN PILOTS ARE SO CONDITIONED TO paved runways that reach halfway to their destination that they give little thought to the possibility of an off-airport emergency landing. But someone makes an emergency or precautionary landing every day. Despite the oft-repeated myth that today's lightplane engines are so highly developed that engine failure is almost unheard of, the fact is that these engines do fail. It has happened to me, and it has happened to colleague Don Downie and his wife Julia (in a brand new airplane!)

Engines fail because something breaks internally when valve heads break off, crankshafts part, or accessory gears are chewed up. Many lightplane engine failures are due to poor or improper maintenance or defective parts, and an amazing number of them are due to the fact that all the gasoline in the airplane's fuel tanks has been replaced by air (FIG. 6-1).

But engine problems are not the only reasons for off-airport landings. Nor are all off-airport landings "forced" landings. Some are precautionary, made in the face of deteriorating weather, or while a small problem, threatening to become worse, is still manageable.

The FAA says that some people are killed or injured in lightplanes because of their reluctance to accept the unpleasant possibilities inherent

Fig. 6-1. Visually check fuel tanks for verification of fuel levels to ensure proper quantity and for verification of fuel color to ensure proper grade.

in airborne emergencies. They say that a desire to save the airplane and an "undue" concern about getting hurt are the factors that lead to indecision and poor decisions when a situation pumps the cockpit ankle deep in adrenaline. In other words, be prepared to meet your responsibilities as pilot in command, and act.

It is possible to plan most of the emergency landing procedure in advance. Make an emergency checklist, keep it handy, and when the time comes, follow it, item by item. Also in advance, learn how various possible landing sites appear from the air at different times of the year. A plowed field is a plowed field, but the color of the soil can differ in different parts of the country, and in the West and Southwest it is often soft with irrigation water. A superficial knowledge of regional agricultural conditions might therefore help in your selection of an emergency landing field and also aid you in deciding whether to land wheels-ups or wheels-down. Cultivated fields are usually satisfactory, and plowed fields are acceptable if the landing is made parallel to the furrows. If landing on an irrigated field, however, a high-wing airplane with gear down will probably end up on its back, so an irrigated field would not be my first choice in a Cessna single.

Without power, it's probably best to look for the biggest field you can find, then consider wind direction (FIG. 6-2). The amount of altitude you have when the fan stops is going to determine how much time you have for the several things that must be done, and several important things will

Fig. 6-2. Engines do quit and force a pilot to draw on all his experience to make a safe emergency landing. The pilot of this restored Spartan C-3 is gliding safely toward a smooth pasture below for a subsequently uneventful landing.

have to wait. You can't select the field from 10,000 feet, and you aren't going to deploy flaps until absolutely certain that you have the field made.

Ground obstructions can make landing into the wind undesirable because they subtract from the available field length; you might not have enough altitude to maneuver for a landing into the wind, and a landing downhill into the wind might be worse than a crosswind or downwind landing. Take the wind if you can get it, but terrain and obstacle considerations come first, as does the simple need to *reach* the selected landing field.

If you have enough altitude, fly a standard traffic pattern, although without power you might want to make a smaller, tighter, and higher pattern than usual. The pattern allows you a good look at the selected field, and it aids in judging distances because it's a familiar procedure. Besides, you'll probably be approaching from downwind anyway, because the selection of a field that is downwind when the emergency develops ensures the maximum distance you can cover before reading the ground, thereby multiplying your options.

FAILED-ENGINE PROCEDURE

Mentioned earlier was the suggestion that you have a plan for in-flight power failure and a prepared checklist to follow. Your first action will always be to establish your most efficient glide speed. From that instant until the airplane comes to a stop on the ground your primary concern is to *fly the airplane*. Depending upon altitude, you then either go through your engine-failure checklist or pick your landing field. Your checklist will start with the application of carburetor heat (with a dead engine, there won't be carb heat for long, and probably not enough to melt carburetor throat ice in any case, but it doesn't do any harm). Check the fuel selector switch, and cycle it to make sure that it rests in the indent it is pointed to and that it is turned to the fullest tank. Turn on the fuel pump, mixture to full rich, and cycle the ignition switch, returning it to BOTH. If the propeller is windmilling, try a shot of primer, and if you have no restart by this time, move the propeller control to low rpm (if appropriate) to minimize drag. Finally, turn the communications radio to 121.5 and squawk 7700 on the transponder.

Your best glide airspeed, that is, the airspeed that will take you the most distance, should be listed on your engine-failure checklist, and you will find it in your owner's manual. If you don't have it, use V_y, your best-rate-of-climb airspeed; it'll be close. V_x will keep you up longer, with the slowest rate-of-descent, but I can think of no use for it until on a short final, under certain conditions.

With your descent speed stabilized, retrim, and then make your call on 121.5: "Mayday, mayday, mayday." Identify the aircraft in the usual way. Then give your position, the nature of your problem, and your intentions. That's all they need. Repeat your call if you have time, and if you have plenty of altitude you might ask for a vector and the distance to the nearest airport. Otherwise, *concentrate on flying your airplane* and keep distractions, including unnecessary conversation with ATC, to a minimum.

It is advisable to keep the speed up until you are sure that you will reach your selected landing patch. High and fast on final is adjustable, but without power there's nothing you can do if you're low and slow. Usually, you will be using short-field technique from that point.

Fig. 6-3. The first rule of an emergency landing is to maintain control of the airplane. Maintain flying speed because an untimely stall during an emergency landing might cause an accident scene similar to this. As long as the cabin remains intact and protects the occupants, the rest of the aircraft is expendable.

Whatever technique the situation dictates, always consider that your airplane is expendable in the interest of occupant protection. The FAA says that, as long as the cabin remains intact, and you strike no immovable object head-on at a significant speed, serious injury is unlikely in a crash (FIG. 6-3).

ENGINE FAILURE ON TAKEOFF

If the engine should fail shortly after liftoff and before you have attained a safe maneuvering altitude—500 feet absolute minimum at V_y in most lightplanes, pattern altitude or 800 feet at V_x—it is inadvisable to attempt to turn back to the field from which you took off. It is usually safer to immediately turn off all electrical, ignition, and fuel switches, establish a glide straight ahead, select a place to land that is no more than 15° to either side of your track, and *concentrate on flying the airplane*. Positive control is your key to an injury-free emergency landing.

The decision to continue straight ahead is often a difficult one, but again, preplanning can help. At your home field, and at others that you regularly visit, study the areas off the ends of the runways and ask yourself where you could land down there if you had to. During the early fall of 1985, I had arranged an interview with Chris Beachner, who was flying a Buick V-8 engine in his homebuilt off the Eloy, Arizona, Municipal Airport. I arrived to discover that Chris had been killed two days before when he attempted a 180-degree turn following engine failure on takeoff. I also recall that, shortly before World War II, my original instructor, along with Tom Braniff's son, were killed when they tried the same thing at Oklahoma City.

The so-called 180-following-engine-failure-soon-after-takeoff has claimed a lot of lives before and since then. In the first place, it is not really a 180. A 180-degree turn would put you parallel to the runway, but not *on* it. To return to the runway, two turns would be required: a 270 and an opposing 90. That's a bit much without power at low altitude. As the record shows, the "180" under these conditions is a trap.

Also keep in mind that, to return to the takeoff field, a downwind turn must be made. That suddenly increases your ground speed, which in turn can easily cause you to hurry the turn, and you know the fatal sequence this can lead to: a hurried turn, crossed controls, low speed, low altitude. . . .

FIRE

The rarest of all forced landings is due to fire. It is also the scariest. A lady I know opened the cabin door of her little Cessna 140 and jumped out onto the runway as smoke came billowing from beneath the engine cowling during the takeoff run. She had just begun to roll and therefore was only bruised and shaken. She had the presence of mind to cut the switch, which saved the airplane. The smoke was generated by a bird's nest erected between two cylinders and a portion of the exhaust manifold.

In-flight fires are practically unheard of because proper maintenance eliminates the causes: leaking fuel lines, cracked manifolds, and accumulations of dirt and oil in the engine compartment. There is nothing in the engine compartment to burn except the fuel being routed through the carburetor and intakes. As long as the connectors and lines are secure and the engine cowling inner surface and firewall are kept clean, the possibility of fire is remote.

If you should experience that one-in-a-million, in-flight fire, your options are obviously limited. Just do as the old-timers did in their more flammable machines: Turn the fuel selector and the master and magneto switches to OFF, and side-slip the airplane to blow the fire away from the cabin. With the fuel supply cut off, there's a good chance that you will blow out the fire and/or starve it. Continue the slip to get on the ground as soon as possible. The side-slip is performed the same as a forward slip, except that you hold the nose a little higher and use rudder to achieve the proper angle.

You understand, I'm working from second-hand intelligence on this subject. I don't even *know* anyone who has ever had an engine fire while flying, except from battle damage in World War II, and the drill then was simply to bail out. But clearly, the way to beat in-flight engine fires in lightplanes is through good maintenance and a thorough inspection prior to the first flight of the day.

Smoke in the cabin during flight is almost always due to an electrical problem, and the commonsense remedy is to cut off all electrics (except the ignition, of course) and land at the nearest airport. Open the storm window and ventilate the cabin. Don't worry about "fanning" the fire; you cannot risk smoke inhalation and the certain loss of control that would bring.

If you carry a fire extinguisher in the airplane, make sure that you know what it contains. Carry only one that uses Halon as an extinguishing agent. This is the least toxic type and is effective against fuel as well as electrical fires. It leaves no residue and will not damage expensive avionics.

By now, it will be hard to find a fabric-covered airplane finished in the old, highly flammable cellulose nitrate dope, so that danger is a thing of the past. Cellulose acetate butyrate dope will burn but won't sustain a live flame in flight.

THE PRECAUTIONARY LANDING

Many people who are now statistics would be alive today had they not been so reluctant to face up to a bad situation and possessed the good sense to make a precautionary landing. I've heard it called a "chicken landing" by some of the hot rocks; but for my part, when I see the choice as being between "stupid" and "chicken," I'd rather be classed as "chicken." I've known some scud-runners and others, including several otherwise very intelligent people, who could never be called "chicken," but they can be called very dead.

Many situations in addition to deteriorating weather, can make it highly desirable to return to earth, posthaste, as they say. These include impending darkness, a dwindling fuel supply, and being "temporarily disoriented," or a combination of these conditions (airborne problems have a way of piling up); it's usually not the first one or two that get you, it's what they lead to, all of which are normally traceable to careless planning.

A precautionary landing is no big deal if you can find an airport close by, which is not too difficult if you have a clue as to where you are. And an off-airport landing *under positive control*, including a slightly bent airplane, sure beats what too often happens when a non-instrument pilot tries to "push the weather" or flies his fuel to exhaustion before looking for a place to land.

A FINAL WORD

The FAA manuals describe how to make power-off emergency landings, but in those examples the airplane is well-positioned when power is retarded, the weather is good, the winds are light, the wind direction is known, and the field selected is large and level with no rocks, trees, or ditches to complicate things. In real life you aren't likely to get all those breaks. The *only* available field from your relatively low altitude might be upwind and reachable, hopefully, by way of a straight-in approach. Most of us find a long straight-in approach more difficult than a final established from well-practiced downwind and base legs, especially when surface wind direction and velocity are uncertain factors.

Also, once the engine develops a terminal case of quiet, the standard short-field technique might be too much of a gamble because you are too close to stalling speed for full flaps on final approach. Without power, $20-25°$ of flaps, along with a minimum airspeed of 1.3 V_{so}, is more practical. Full flaps pitch the nose down too steeply, and the airplane will stop flying too suddenly at the stall. Without power you are much better off to be a few knots too fast because *positive control* is your single most important consideration. To put it another way, it's better to run into obstacles at the far end of the field at 10 knots than to smash into them at the approach end at 50 knots.

STAY WITH THE AIRCRAFT

Two recent airline accidents revealed the importance of flying and landing the aircraft without panic during an emergency; managing the situation without losing control of the aircraft. The April 1988 Aloha Airlines accident and the July 1989 United Airlines accident were less serious than they could have been because each pilot did a remarkable job of controlling their respective aircraft to emergency landings at airports.

An Aloha Airlines 737 was en route from Hilo to Honolulu, Hawaii, when the aircraft fuselage skin ruptured at 24,000 feet, pulling one flight attendant out of the cabin; the flight attendant would be the only death. The skin failure rapidly opened a gaping hole that extended 15 to 20 feet over six rows of passenger seats. A number of passengers held on to a flight attendant for the remainder of the trip to prevent a second loss of life. The flight carried 89 passengers and a crew of six.

First Officer Madeline Tompkins was flying the aircraft at the time of the decompression; Captain Robert Schornstheimer, who had flown for Aloha Airlines for 10 years, took over the controls and chose Kahuhai Airport for an emergency landing. Fifteen minutes later the aircraft arrived at the airport for the emergency landing. Witnesses who work at the airport were amazed to see the aircraft execute the landing approach with a large portion of the fuselage missing and one engine on fire. Schornstheimer landed the 737 without further loss of life.

It was subsequently determined that corrosion had caused the skin to rupture, and the accident brought the aging aircraft issue into the national spotlight. General aviation aircraft came away relatively unscathed because most light aircraft are not subject to the pressurization-depressurization cycles of air carrier aircraft.

Perhaps the most heroic job of saving an aircraft after a catastrophic incident occurred when a turbine disk in a DC-10 engine disintegrated, broke away, and severed the aircraft hydraulic lines, resulting in total loss of hydraulic pressure; the DC-10 requires hydraulic pressure to operate the primary control surfaces. Captain Alfred Haynes had been flying for United for 33 years; he reported the loss of hydraulic pressure to ATC one minute after the engine failed. Initially the aircraft was headed for an emergency landing at Dubuque, Iowa, but was forced to head for Sioux City, Iowa, due to the graveness of the situation.

Off-duty United Captain Dennis Fitch joined Haynes and First Officer William Records in the cockpit to help handle the only flight controls available: throttles of the two remaining engines. Second Officer Dudley Dvorak monitored conditions in the back of the aircraft. The aircraft could only make wide right-hand turns during the descent. Haynes had hoped to land on a 9,000-foot-long runway at Sioux City, but had to opt for a shorter 6,000-foot runway to take advantage of the aircraft's position relative to the airport.

The aircraft was surprisingly straight-and-level on short approach when the right wing dipped and struck the ground, causing the aircraft to cartwheel down the runway and across the airport; 110 passengers and crew members died and 186 survived, including the cockpit crew. (A television news crew taped the impact from behind an airport chainlink fence.)

Both accidents demonstrate that a landing can be executed under the worst imaginable emergency conditions. The 737 had to be handled gingerly in flight and upon landing to prevent separation or folding at the section of missing fuselage; the DC-10 was balanced between two engines that were jockeyed with engine thrust to maintain at least a limited sense of controlled flight. In both cases, the pilot and cockpit crew of the aircraft stayed with the crippled aircraft and saved many lives.

7
Communicate

EVERYBODY CAN REMEMBER FOULED-UP SITUATIONS THAT WERE caused by poor communications. One of my favorite examples happened during World War II. A Navy student pilot reported that he had seen an N3N trainer, buzz number so-and-so, making an emergency landing in a farm field approximately 20 miles from the naval air station. The downed pilot's instructor, one of those I-can-fly-a-barn-door-if-it's-got-an-engine types, climbed into another N3N and flew to the site of the forced landing to assess the damage and retrieve his student.

Upon arrival, the instructor was dismayed to find the disabled airplane in an incredibly small field that was bounded by a low rock fence. He circled, noting that a much larger field was adjacent to the one containing the downed aircraft, which, by the way, was clearly undamaged. The instructor gave scant consideration to the obviously more appropriate field. If that solo student could squeeze an N3N into such a space....

Well, you guessed it; the instructor smashed a wing into the rock fence opposite his touchdown point as he attempted a last-second ground loop to avoid striking the fence head-on.

He climbed from the cockpit and strode purposefully toward his student. "Mister," he said, struggling to control himself. "Tell me exactly how you managed to land in this (expletive deleted) pea patch?"

"I didn't exactly land here, sir." The student gestured toward the adjacent field. "I landed over there and sort of bounced over here."

That instructor could have avoided the damage to his airplane and embarrassment to himself had he bothered to seek additional details of the forced landing from the cadet who reported it, or by radio from the one who performed it. A little communication would have made a lot of difference.

On a more somber note, I'm reminded of the 1977 collision between two Boeing 747s that killed 582 people on a fog-shrouded runway at Tenerife in the Canary Islands. That one happened because both captains believed they had been cleared for takeoff. One had not been cleared.

So, the kind of communication I am talking about here implies complete understanding, among the crew members, and between the crew and the controlling authorities on the ground. Specifically, we are concerned with communications attendant to airport and traffic pattern operations in visual meteorological conditions. By extension, that might include flight planning, but I will focus on the use of the aircraft radio: whom to call, when, how, and why.

RADIO PHRASEOLOGY

The "how" means the use of acceptable phraseology as well as tuning the proper frequency. It's true that controllers would rather hear from a pilot who stumbles through a radio transmission, repeating himself and tying up the frequency for several minutes with a message that could have been given in five to 10 seconds, than not hear from him at all. But the pilot who has thus identified himself as an inconsiderate amateur is increasingly, these days, receiving less and less consideration from busy controllers. Although he might meet the legal requirements for entry into a TCA, a busy controller might tell him to remain clear of the TCA, not only to free the radio frequency, but to avoid mixing a pilot of questionable ability with the other traffic. Mostly, it is because the controller lacks the time to bother with the pilot who has failed to learn the proper use of his communications radio.

There are those who take the position that their tax money is paying for the air traffic control system, including controllers' salaries, and therefore the burden is on the controllers to "do their jobs." That isn't exactly the way it is. First of all, your relationship with the controllers is 50-50; you do your share, they do their share. The system will not work without pilot cooperation (FIG. 7-1). Secondly, while it is true that the controller is there to serve you, he or she is also there to serve all those

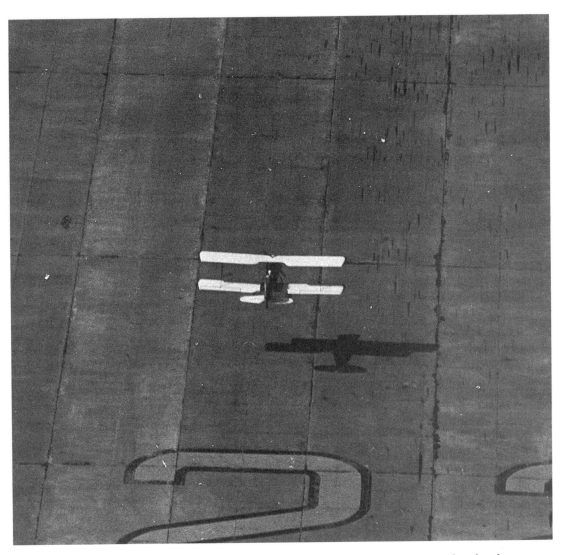

Fig. 7-1. A restored Meyers OTW biplane without a transceiver is permitted to land at a controlled airport for static display during a fly-in because the pilot telephoned ahead. Controllers knew when to expect the Meyers and cleared it to land by displaying proper light gun signals.

other taxpayers who have radios in their airplanes. Once again, the key is courtesy and consideration for the other guy. And, once again, that translates into safe flying.

Pilots often do not use the FAA-recommended phraseology when using their communication radios but employ something close that has gained acceptance because it is brief and because controllers understand it. An example is reference to altitudes. While the controller will say, for example, "five thousand five hundred" or "eight thousand five hundred," many pilots will say, "five point five" or "eight point five," which the controllers seem to accept without complaint. But someday, there is bound to be a fatal misunderstanding as a result of such inventiveness; not because it is not sufficiently descriptive, but because pilot and controller are assigning different terms to a common concept.

The term "over" isn't heard much anymore. It means that your message is complete and that you expect a reply. The nature of your message is usually enough to establish whether of not a reply is expected. If you think there could be any doubt, add "over" at the end.

Never acknowledge a controller's directive with a simple "Roger." The controller might be in contact with several aircraft, and he or she has no way of knowing whose "Roger" it is. Acknowledge with the aircraft type (Cessna, Cherokee, etc.) and the last three digits of the N-number (assuming that your initial contact included the complete N-number, and that the controller has responded to you using the abbreviated call sign). Otherwise, use your complete N-number, because the controller apparently is in contact with an aircraft using an N-number that could be confused with yours.

Never hesitate to ask a controller to "say again" if you do not completely understand a directive. As always, a little common sense goes a long way. If, for example, Ground Control has directed you to a runway for takeoff that is reached by crossing another runway, make sure that you understand that message. If there is any doubt at all, repeat the taxi instructions back to the controller. Never allow your desire for brevity to compromise total understanding between you and a controller. You don't have to get smashed crossing that intervening runway in order to regret that you did not clarify your instructions. Taxiing across a runway without a controller's permission can get you into serious trouble with the FAA.

Begin each transmission with the name of the facility being called:

- Approach Control—"Albuquerque Approach"

- Ground Control—"Wichita Ground"

- Control Tower—"Lawton Tower"

- Flight service station—"Hanford Radio"

- Unicom—"Hobart Unicom"

The name of the facility being called is immediately followed by the identification, which is the aircraft type and its N-number, followed by the request:

"Wichita Ground, Cessna Five Niner Two Seven Juliet, at Yingling Aircraft, taxi to Learjet."

You told him where you are and that you want to taxi around the terminal to the north edge of the airport where Learjet is located. Had you been ready to depart the airport and needed taxi instructions to the proper runway, you would have said:

"Wichita Ground, Cessna Five Niner Two Seven Juliet, at Yingling Aircraft, ready to taxi, VFR to Dallas, with Information Foxtrot."

"Foxtrot," for "F" in the phonetic air radiotelephone alphabet, is the coded age of the automatic terminal information service (ATIS) broadcast. ATIS is a recording by tower personnel, transmitted continuously that provides basic airport and meteorological data at major airports. It is normally updated each hour, and each succeeding ATIS advances one letter. When you tell the controller which ATIS you have monitored, Foxtrot, in the above example, the controller knows whether or not you have the latest one.

Typically, an ATIS broadcast provides the time (UTC or Zulu), ceiling and visibility (if better than 5,000 feet and five miles, visibility might be omitted), obstructions to visibility, temperature and dew point, wind, altimeter setting, runways in use, curring NOTAMs, plus AIRMETs and SIGMETs in adverse weather. The purpose of these recordings is to free the controllers from the need to repeat this data for each arriving and departing aircraft, giving them more time to ensure the safe separation of the air traffic.

The ATIS radio frequencies are shown on sectional charts just below the control tower frequencies.

Ground Control frequencies are not shown on sectionals. Obtain them from the flight service station specialist during the weather briefing, from the FBO when you pay your bill, or preferably, from the *Airport/ Facility Directory (A/FD)*. Normally, Ground Control will be in the 121.6 through 121.9 band. After landing, tower will usually supply the Ground Control frequency. Do not leave the tower frequency until told to do so.

UNCONTROLLED AIRPORTS

Takeoff from an airport that has no tower does not relieve you of the need to communicate. Always use the common traffic advisory frequency (CTAF) listed in the *A/FD*. If there is a flight service station on the field, the CTAF will probably be 123.6. If there is no flight service station, the CTAF will usually be the unicom frequency (it's on the sectional charts and will be in the band width of 122.7 through 123.0 inclusive). If there is no tower, no flight service station, and no unicom, transmit your intentions on multicom (122.9). If the tower is closed, the CTAF will usually be the tower frequency. The important thing is to let other air traffic in the area know what you are doing, that is, where you are and where you intend to be in that shared airspace.

How can you be sure that whatever traffic is out there is guarding the proper frequency? You cannot, but that does not relieve your obligation to operate safely. Besides, the pilot who *is* monitoring your call might be the one who didn't see you in the pattern.

When approaching a field that has no tower, tune to the appropriate CTAF about 10 to 15 miles out. You might hear others operating from the field and learn the wind and active runway. Then you can announce your own position and intentions. If there is a unicom or flight service station on the field, obtain local airport advisories: runway, wind, altimeter, and known traffic. If the unicom does not reply, transmit in the blind (the FAA calls it "self-announce," which makes no sense), and address the transmission to "Traffic." For example, "Hobart Traffic, Cessna Five Niner Two Seven Juliet, ten miles southeast at two thousand five hundred. Will enter pattern upwind for Runway Three Six, Hobart."

As you enter the pattern (anyone already in the pattern has the right-of-way), identify yourself and give your position and intentions once again. Do this whether or not there is any other traffic. The fact that you don't see any traffic is all the more reason to keep the world informed of your presence and intentions.

Report your turn from downwind to base leg, from base to final, and, once on the ground, again transmit your identity and position. If the airport is small and you have to back-taxi on the active runway, make position reports entering and exiting the active runway.

CONTROLLED AIRPORTS

Every airport that has an operating control tower automatically has an airport traffic area (ATA) surrounding it that always has a radius of five statute miles from the center of the airport and extends upward to, but not including, 3,000 feet agl. When the tower is not in operation, the ATA does not exist. ATAs are not shown on charts. You must be in radio contact with the tower in order to enter an ATA, and you should make your initial call at least 10 miles from the ATA.

CONTROL ZONES

Control zones (CZs) are shown on sectional charts. They vary in shape (many have the shape of a keyhole) because they include extensions for IFR arrivals and departures. CZs extend upward to 14,500 feet, the base of the continental control area, and many surround airports that have no control towers, but a flight service station or weather reporting station. You must obtain a special VFR clearance to enter a control zone when the ceiling is less than 1,000 feet and/or the visibility is less than three miles.

TRSAs, ARSAs, TCAs

The air traffic control system in the United States is a patchwork of add-on rules and procedures. Year by year, controlled airspace is added on, new regulations are added on, and new technology is added on. There has never been an overall, integrated plan. That's bound to spawn some confusion.

The terminal radar service area (TRSA) imposes no restrictions for VFR aircraft. It is simply an optional radar service for VFR pilots provided, according to the FAA, only on a "controller workload permitting" basis. The TRSA as presently offered is more confusin' than amusin'. On aeronautical charts, it is indicated by a set of solid magenta concentric "quasi-circles" (FIG. 7-2). TRSAs are being replaced by ARSAs in many locations.

The airport radar service area (ARSA), shown on aeronautical charts by slashed magenta circles (FIG. 7-3), consists of two circular blocks of airspace normally 4,000 feet in height, centered over the airport, and is perhaps best understood by referencing the FAA drawing (FIG. 7-4). The inner circle has a radius of five nautical miles and begins at the surface. The outer circle has a radius of 10 nautical miles and begins at 1,200 feet above the surface. An "outer area" possessing a radius of 20 nautical miles surrounds the two smaller blocks of airspace.

The terminal control area (TCA) is always described as resembling an upside-down wedding cake, sometimes with a slice or two taken from it. Each circular layer of airspace, although larger in diameter than the one below it, might not be perfectly round. You must reference your sectional chart for a general view of each TCA, and then study the special

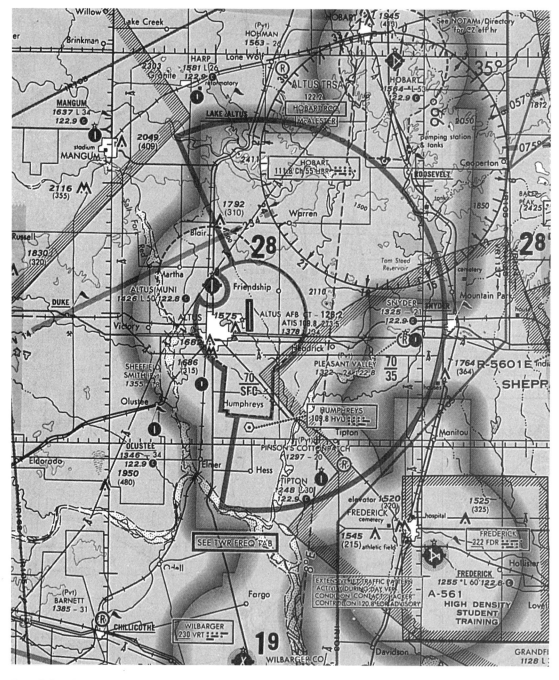

Fig. 7-2. The Altus, Oklahoma, terminal radar service area (TRSA) envelops airspace at Altus Air Force Base. The inner portion extends from the surface up to 7,000 feet, and the outer portion extends from 3,500 feet up to 7,000 feet. Altus Municipal Airport is outside the TRSA.

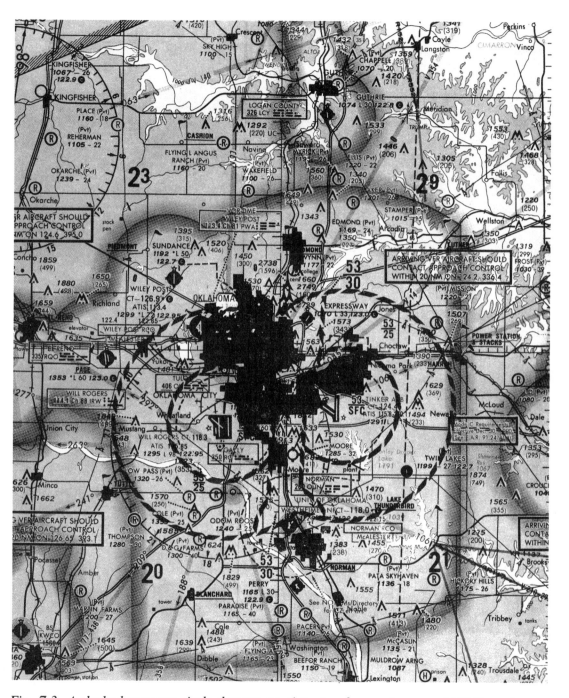

Fig. 7-3. A slashed magenta circle denotes an airport radar service area (ARSA) on the sectional map.

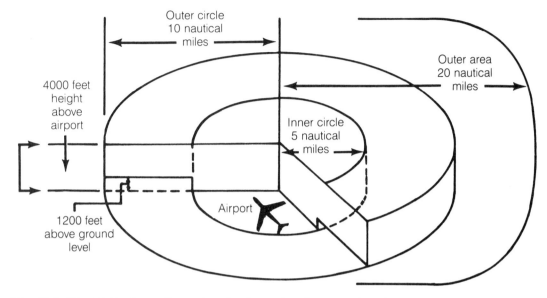

Fig. 7-4. The FAA's three-dimensional schematic of a typical ARSA.

Terminal Area Charts in order to determine the dimensions of each layer. TCAs are not standardized. The top layer of TCA airspace is, of course, the largest and caps all the rest.

On sectionals, TCAs are indicated by solid blue lines (FIG. 7-5).

Currently, the requirements for entering a TCA are a 4096-code transponder with Mode C, a VOR receiver, and an operating two-way radio with all the necessary ATC frequencies. To land or depart the primary TCA airport, the pilot must hold at least a private pilot certificate.

These are the *minimum* requirements. Then *if* you sound as if you know what you are doing when you contact the tower, the controller might clear you to enter the TCA. After that, you must be able to fly the airplane with a reasonable degree of precision and employ the proper aviation radio phraseology.

RADIO PROCEDURES FOR ENTERING THE TCA

When the destination is the major terminal underlying a TCA, make your initial radio call the Approach Control while still outside the TCA. Do not penetrate any layer of the TCA until you are cleared to do so. The top layer of the TCA might be 20 miles or so from the airport. Note that the top layer of the Dallas TCA (FIG. 7-5) is 40 nautical miles across and has an upper limit of 8,000 feet and a floor of 5,000 feet, except for a hunk on the north edge that has a floor of 4,000 feet. Little bits of the first

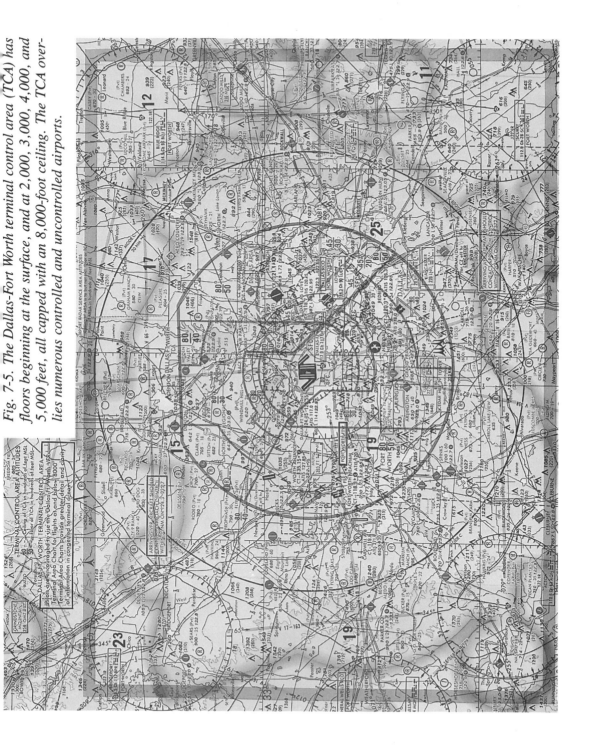

Fig. 7-5. The Dallas-Fort Worth terminal control area (TCA) has floors beginning at the surface, and at 2,000, 3,000, 4,000, and 5,000 feet, all capped with an 8,000-foot ceiling. The TCA overlies numerous controlled and uncontrolled airports.

layer atop the core have a floor of 2,000 feet, while the odd-shaped layer above it appears to have a floor of 3,000 feet, and the southeast quadrant has another piece of airspace with a 4,000-foot floor.

Perhaps you can tell from this example why pilots who fly only occasionally to major terminals have trouble figuring out just where in the hell the TCA floors and outer limits happen to be. Clearly, the safest procedure is to make your initial call while still outside the lateral limits of the top layer.

Approach Control will vector you into the TCA until the tower controller takes over to give pattern and landing directives. Tower in turn will hand you off the Ground Control when you are down and on the taxiway. Do not change radio frequencies until told to do so. Most ground control frequencies are in the 121.6 through 121.9 bandwidth; therefore many controllers will omit the numbers preceding the decimal point. For 121.7 the controller might say, "Contact Ground point seven." Tower and Approach Control frequencies are on sectionals and terminal area charts.

Appendix A
Selected Abbreviations, FAR Part 1

"ADF" means automatic direction finder.

"AGL" means above ground level.

"ALS" means approach light system.

"ASR" means airport surveillance radar.

"ATC" means air traffic control.

"CAS" means calibrated airspeed.

"CAT II" means Category II.

"DH" means decision height.

"DME" means distance measuring equipment compatible with TACAN.

"FAA" means Federal Aviation Administration.

"GS" means glide slope.

"HIRL" means high-intensity runway light system.

"IAS" means indicated airspeed.

"IFR" means instrument flight rules.

"ILS" means instrument landing system.

"IM" means ILS inner marker.

"INT" means intersection.

"LDA" means localizer-type directional aid.

"LMM" means compass locator at the middle marker.

"LOC" means ILS localizer.

"LOM" means compass locator at the outer marker.

"MAA" means maximum authorized IFR altitude.

"MALS" means medium intensity approach light system.

"MALSR" means medium intensity approach light system with runway alignment indicator lights.

"MCA" means minimum crossing altitude.

"MDA" means minimum descent altitude.

"MEA" means minimum en route IFR altitude.

"MM" means ILS middle marker.

"MOCA" means minimum obstruction clearance altitude.

"MRA" means minimum reception altitude.

"MSL" means mean sea level.

"NDB" means nondirectional beacon.

"NOPT" means no procedure turn required.

"OM" means outer marker.

"PAR" means precision approach radar.

"RAIL" means runway alignment indicator light system.

"RCLM" means runway centerline marking.

"RCLS" means runway centerline light system.

"REIL" means runway end identification lights.

"RVR" means runway visual range as measured in the touch-down area.

"SALS" means short approach light system.

"SSALS" means simplified short approach light system.

"SSALSR" means simplified short approach light system with runway alignment indicator lights plus coffee and doughnuts.

"TACAN" means ultra-high frequency tactical air navigation air.

"TAS" means true airspeed.

"TCAS" means traffic alert and collision avoidance system.

"TDZL" means touchdown zone lights.

"TVOR" means very high frequency terminal omnirange station.

"V_a" means design maneuvering speed.

"V_b" means design speed for maximum gust intensity.

"V_c" means design cruising speed.

"V_d" means design diving speed.

"V_{df}/M_{df}" means demonstrated flight diving speed.

"V_f" means design flap speed.

"V_{fc}/M_{fc}" means maximum speed for stability characteristics.

"V_{fe}" means maximum flap extended speed.

"V_h" means maximum speed in level flight with maximum continuous power.

"V_{le}" means maximum landing gear extended speed.

"V_{lo}" means maximum landing gear operating speed.

"V_{lof}" means liftoff speed.

"V_{mc}" means minimum control speed with the critical engine inoperative.

"V_{mo}/M_{mo}" means maximum operating limit speed.

"V_{mu}" means minimum unstick speed.

"V_{ne}" means never exceed speed.

"V_{no}" means maximum structural cruising speed.

"V_r" means rotation speed.

"V_s" means the stalling speed or the minimum steady flight speed at which the airplane is controllable.

"V_{so}" means the stalling speed or the minimum steady flight speed in the landing configuration.

"V_{s1}" means the stalling speed or the minimum steady flight speed obtained in a specific configuration.

"V_x" means speed for the best angle of climb.

"V_y" means speed for the best rate of climb.

"V_1" means takeoff decision speed (formerly denoted as critical engine failure speed).

"V_2" means takeoff safety speed.

"V_{2min}" means minimum takeoff safety speed.

"VFR" means visual flight rules.

"VHF" means very high frequency.

"VOR" means very high frequency omnirange station.

"VORTAC" means co-located VOR and TACAN.

Appendix B
Selected Definitions, FAR Part 1

Airport traffic area means, unless otherwise specifically designated in Part 93, that airspace within a horizontal radius of five statute miles from the geographical center of any airport at which a control tower is operating, extending from the surface up to, but not including, 3,000 feet above the elevation of the airport.

Air traffic clearance means an authorization by air traffic control, for the purpose of preventing collision between known aircraft, for an aircraft to proceed under specified traffic conditions within controlled airspace.

Alternate airport means an airport at which an aircraft may land if a landing at the intended airport becomes inadvisable.

Calibrated airspeed means the indicated airspeed of an aircraft, corrected for position and instrument error. Calibrated airspeed is equal to true airspeed in standard atmosphere at sea level.

Category—

(1) As used with respect to the certification, ratings, privileges, and limitations of airmen, means a broad classification of aircraft. Examples include: airplane, rotorcraft, glider, and lighter-than-air; and

(2) As used with the respect to the certification of aircraft, means a grouping of aircraft based upon intended use or operating limitations. Examples include: transport, normal, utility, aerobatic, limited, restricted, and provisional.

Category II operations, with respect to the operation of aircraft, means a straight-in ILS approach to the runway of an airport under a Category II ILS instrument approach procedure issued by the Administrator or other appropriate authority.

Category III operations, with respect to the operation of aircraft, means an ILS approach to, and landing on, the runway of an airport using a Category III ILS instrument approach procedure issued by the Administrator or other appropriate authority.

Ceiling means the height above the earth's surface of the lowest layer of clouds or obscuring phenomena that is reported as "broken," "overcast," or "obscuration," and not classified as "thin" or "partial."

Class—

(1) As used with respect to the certification, ratings, privileges, and limitations of airmen, means a classification of aircraft within a category having similar operating characteristics. Examples include: single-engine; multi-engine; land; water; gyroplane; helicopter; airship; and free balloon; and

(2) As used with respect to the certification of aircraft, means a broad grouping of aircraft having similar characteristics of propulsion, flight, or landing. Examples include: airplane; rotorcraft; glider; balloon; landplane; and seaplane.

Controlled airspace means airspace designated as a continental control area, control area, control zone, terminal control area, or transition area, within which some or all aircraft may be subject to air traffic control.

Decision height, with respect to the operation of aircraft, means the height at which a decision must be made, during an ILS or PAR instrument approach, to either continue the approach or to execute a missed approach.

Flap extended speed means the highest speed permissible with wing flaps in a prescribed extended position.

Flight level means a level of constant atmospheric pressure related to a reference datum of 29.92 inches of mercury (Hg). Each is stated in three digits that represent hundreds of feet. For example, flight level 250 represents a barometric altimeter indication of 25,000 feet, flight level 255, an indication of 25,500 feet.

Flight visibility means the average forward horizontal distance, from the cockpit of an aircraft in flight, at which prominent, unlighted objects may be seen and identified by day and prominent lighted objects may be seen and identified by night.

Ground visibility means prevailing horizontal visibility near the earth's surface as reported by the United States National Weather Service or an accredited observer.

IFR conditions means weather conditions below the minimum for flight under visual flight rules. ["IMC" for instrument meteorological conditions, apparently borrowed from the British, is currently fashionable. It means the same as IFR conditions.]

Indicated airspeed means the speed of an aircraft as shown on its pitot static airspeed indicator calibrated to reflect standard atmosphere adiabatic compressible flow at sea level, uncorrected for airspeed system errors.

Landing gear extended speed means the maximum speed at which an aircraft can be safely flown with the landing gear extended.

Landing gear operating speed means the maximum speed at which the landing gear can be safely extended or retracted.

Large aircraft means aircraft of more than 12,500 pounds maximum certificated takeoff weight.

Lighter-than-air aircraft means aircraft that can rise and remain suspended by using contained gas weighing less than the air that is displaced by the gas.

Load factor means the ratio of a specified load to the total weight of the aircraft. The specified load is expressed in terms of any of the following: aerodynamic forces, inertia forces, or ground or water reactions.

Mach number means the ratio of true airspeed to the speed of sound.

Manifold pressure means absolute pressure as measured at the appropriate point in the induction system, and usually expressed in inches of mercury.

Minimum descent altitude means the lowest altitude, expressed in feet above mean sea level, to which descent is authorized on final approach or during circle-to-land maneuvering in execution of a standard instrument approach procedure, where no electronic glide slope is provided.

Navigable airspace means airspace at and above the minimum flight altitudes prescribed by or under this chapter [Part 1], including airspace needed for safe takeoff and landing.

Night means the time between the end of evening civil twilight and the beginning of morning civil twilight, as published in the American Air Almanac, converted to local time. [If you are a fan of "Frank and Ernest" in the Sunday comics, then you know that "midnight is when the darkness is directly overhead."]

Nonprecision approach procedure means a standard instrument approach procedure in which no electronic glide slope is provided.

Over-the-top means above the layer of clouds or other obscuring phenomena forming the ceiling.

Pilotage means navigation by visual reference to landmarks.

Pilot in command means the pilot responsible for the operation and safety of an aircraft during flight time.

Precision approach procedure means a standard instrument approach procedure in which an electronic glide slope is provided, such as ILS and PAR.

Rated maximum continuous power with respect to reciprocating, turbopropeller, and turboshaft engines, means the approved brake horsepower that is developed statically or in flight, in standard atmosphere at a specified altitude, within the engine operating limitations established under Part 33, and approved for unrestricted periods of use.

Rated takeoff power, with respect to reciprocating, turbopropeller, and turboshaft engine type certification, means the approved brake horsepower that is developed statically under standard sea level conditions established under Part 33, and limited in use to periods of not over five minutes for takeoff operation.

Rating means a statement that, as a part of a certificate, sets forth special conditions, privileges, or limitations.

Reporting point means a geographical location in relation to which the position of an aircraft is reported.

Restricted area means airspace designated under Part 73 within which the flight of aircraft, while not wholly prohibited, is subject to restriction.

RNAV way point (W/P) means a predetermined geographical position used for route or instrument approach definition or progress reporting purposes that is defined relative to a VORTAC station position.

Sea level engine means a reciprocating aircraft engine having a rated takeoff power that is attainable only at sea level.

Small aircraft means aircraft of 12,500 pounds or less, maximum certified takeoff weight.

Standard atmosphere means the atmosphere defined in U.S. Standard Atmosphere, 1962 (Geopotential altitude tables).

Stopway means an area beyond the takeoff runway, no less wide than the runway, and centered upon the extended centerline of the runway, able to support the airplane during an aborted takeoff, without causing structural damage to the airplane, and designated by the airport authorities for use in decelerating the airplane during an aborted takeoff.

Takeoff power—

(1) With respect to reciprocating engines, means the brake horsepower that is developed under standard sea-level conditions, and under the maximum conditions of crankshaft rotational speed and engine manifold pressure approved for the normal takeoff, and limited in continuous use to the period of time shown in the approved engine specification; and

(2) With respect to turbine engines, means the brake horsepower that is developed under static conditions at a specified altitude and atmospheric temperature, and under the maximum conditions of rotor shaft rotational speed and gas temperature approved for the normal takeoff, and limited in continuous use to the period of time shown in the approved engine specification.

True airspeed means the airspeed of the aircraft relative to undisturbed air.

Traffic pattern means the traffic flow that is prescribed for aircraft landing at, taxiing on, or taking off from an airport.

Type—

(1) As used with respect to the certification, ratings, privileges, and limitations of airmen, means a specific make and basic model of aircraft, including modifications thereto that do not change its handling or flight characteristics. Examples include: DC-7, 1049, and F-27; and

(2) As used with respect to the certification of aircraft, means those aircraft that are similar in design. Examples include: DC-7 and DC-7C, 1049G and 1049H; and F-27 and F-27F.

VFR over-the-top, with respect to the operation of aircraft, means the operation of an aircraft over-the-top under VFR when it is not being operated on an IFR flight plan.

Appendix C
Pilot/Controller Glossary (Abridged)

THIS APPENDIX IS A COMPILATION OF DEFINITIONS FROM THE *Airman's Information Manual*. The majority of the terms defined are of special interest to the pilot when taking off and landing. Many terms that apply to en route flying, instrument flying, and other specialized areas have been deleted.

Terms and phrases that are spoken by controller or pilot start with a capital letter. Ellipses follow the spoken terms, for instance: Maintain....

Certain definitions have been paraphrased and edited for style and clarity. Every effort has been made to retain the FAA's intent, but any pilot who would like to review a complete definition and all glossary terms should consult the AIM.

Abeam....—An aircraft is abeam a fix, point, or object when that fix, point or object is approximately 90 degrees to the right or left of the aircraft track. Abeam indicates a general position, rather than a precise location.

Abort....—To terminate a preplanned aircraft maneuver, such as to abort a takeoff.

Acknowledge....—Let me know that you have received my message.

additional services—Advisory information that is provided by ATC that includes, but is not limited to, eight situations:

1. Traffic advisories.
2. Vectors, when requested by the pilot, to assist aircraft receiving traffic advisories to avoid observed traffic.
3. Altitude deviation information of 300 feet or more from an assigned altitude as observed on a verified (reading correctly) automatic altitude readout (Mode C).
4. Advisories that traffic is no longer a factor.
5. Weather and chaff information.
6. Weather assistance.
7. Bird activity information.
8. Holding pattern surveillance.

Additional services are provided to the extent possible contingent only upon the controller's capability to fit them into the performance of higher priority duties and on the basis of limitations of the radar, volume of traffic, frequency congestion, and controller workload. The controller has complete discretion for determining if he is able to provide or continue to provide a service in a particular case. The controller's reason not to provide or continue to provide a service in a particular case is not subject to question by the pilot and need not be made known to him.

administrator—The Federal Aviation Administrator or any person to whom he has delegated his authority in the matter concerned.

Advise intentions....—Tell me what you plan to do.

advisory—Advice and information provided to assist pilots in the safe conduct of flight and aircraft movement.

advisory frequency—The appropriate frequency to be used for airport advisory service.

advisory service—Advice and information provided by a facility to assist pilots in the safe conduct of flight and aircraft movement.

aircraft—Device that is used or intended to be used for flight in the air, and when used in air traffic control terminology, may include the flight crew.

aircraft classes—For the purposes of wake turbulence separation minima, ATC classifies aircraft:

- Heavy is aircraft capable of takeoff weights of 300,000 pounds or more, whether or not they are operating at this weight during a particular phase of flight.
- Large is aircraft of more than 12,500 pounds, maximum certificated takeoff weight, up to 300,000 pounds.
- Small is aircraft of 12,500 pounds or less maximum certificated takeoff weight.

airport advisory area—The area within 10 miles of an airport without a control tower or where the tower is not in operation, and on which a flight service station is located.

airport advisory service—A service provided by flight service stations or the military at airports not serviced by an operating control tower. This service consists of providing information to arriving and departing aircraft concerning wind direction and speed, favored runway, altimeter setting, pertinent known traffic, pertinent known field conditions, airport taxi routes, traffic patterns, and authorized instrument approach procedures. This information is advisory in nature and does not constitute clearance.

airport elevation/field elevation—The highest point on an airport's usable runways, measured in feet from mean sea level.

airport marking aids—Markings used on runway and taxiway surfaces to identify a specific runway, a runway threshold, a centerline, a hold line, and the like. A runway should be marked in accordance with its present usages, such as visual, nonprecision instrument, and precision instrument.

approach control facility—A terminal facility that provides approach control service in a terminal area.

approach control service—Air traffic control service provided by an approach control facility for arriving and departing VFR/IFR aircraft and, on occasion, en route aircraft. At certain airports not served by an approach control facility, the air route traffic control center provides limited approach control service.

approach speed—The recommended speed contained in aircraft manuals used by pilots when making an approach to landing. This speed will vary for different segments of an approach as well as for aircraft weight and configuration.

arrival time—The time an aircraft touches down on arrival.

ATC instructions—Directives issued by air traffic control for the purpose of requiring a pilot to take specific actions.

base leg—A flight path at right angles to the landing runway off its approach end. The base leg normally extends from the downwind leg to the intersection of the extended runway centerline.

Cleared for takeoff....—ATC authorization for an aircraft to depart. It is predicated on known traffic and known physical airport conditions.

Cleared for the option....—ATC authorization for an aircraft to make a touch-and-go, low approach, missed approach, stop and go, or full-stop landing at the discretion of the pilot. It is normally used in training so that an instructor can evaluate a student's performance under changing conditions.

Cleared through....—ATC authorization for an aircraft to make intermediate stops at specified airports without refiling a flight plan while en route to the clearance limit.

Cleared to land....—ATC authorization for an aircraft to land. It is predicated on known traffic and known physical airport conditions.

closed runway—A runway that is unusable for aircraft operations. Only the airport management or military operations office can close a runway.

closed traffic—Successive operations involving takeoffs and landings or low approaches where the aircraft does not exit the traffic pattern.

common traffic advisory frequency (CTAF)—A frequency designed for the purpose of carrying out airport advisory practices while operating to or from an uncontrolled airport. The CTAF might be a unicom, multicom, FSS, or tower frequency and is identified in appropriate aeronautical publications.

controlled airspace—Airspace designated as a control zone, airport radar service area, terminal control area, transition area, control area, continental control area, or positive control area within which selected or all aircraft might be subject to air traffic control.

course—The intended direction of flight in the horizontal plane, measured in degrees from north.

crosswind—Regarding the traffic pattern, the word means "crosswind leg." Regarding wind conditions, the word means a wind not parallel to the runway or the path of an aircraft.

crosswind component—The wind component measured in knots at 90 degrees to the longitudinal axis of the runway.

crosswind leg—A flight path at right angles to the landing runway off its upwind end.

departure control—A function of an approach control facility providing air traffic control service for departing and, under certain conditions, VFR aircraft.

departure time—The time an aircraft becomes airborne.

displaced threshold—A threshold that is located at a point on the runway other than the designated beginning of the runway.

distress—A condition of being threatened by serious and/or imminent danger and of requiring immediate assistance.

downburst—A strong downdraft that induces an outburst of damaging winds on or near the ground. Damaging winds, either straight or curved, are highly divergent. The sizes of downbursts vary from one-half mile or less, to more than 10 miles. An intense downburst often causes widespread damage. Damaging wind lasting five to 30 minutes could reach speeds as high as 120 knots.

downwind leg—A flight path parallel to the landing runway in the direction opposite to landing. The downwind leg normally extends between the crosswind leg and the base leg.

emergency—A distress or an urgency condition.

Expedite....—Used by an air traffic controller when prompt compliance is required to avoid the development of an imminent situation.

Final....—Commonly used to mean that an aircraft is on the final approach or is aligned with a landing area.

final approach—A flight path in the direction of landing along the extended runway centerline. The final approach normally extends from the base leg to the runway. An aircraft making a straight-in approach VFR is also considered to be on final approach.

flight path—A line, course, or track along which an aircraft is flying or intended to be flown.

Fly heading (in degrees)....—Informs the pilot of the heading he should fly. The pilot might have to turn to, or continue on, a specific compass direction in order to comply with the instructions. The pilot is expected to turn in the shorter direction to the heading unless otherwise instructed by an air traffic controller.

glide slope or **glide path**—Provides vertical guidance for aircraft during approach and landing. Either is based on, among other things, visual ground aids, such as a vertical approach slope indicator (VASI), that provide vertical guidance for VFR approach or for the visual portion of an instrument approach and landing.

Go ahead....—Proceed with your message. Not to be used for any other purpose.

Go around....—Instructions for a pilot to abandon his approach to landing. Additional instructions might follow. Unless otherwise instructed by an air traffic controller, a VFR aircraft or an aircraft conducting a visual approach should overfly the runway while climbing to traffic pattern altitude and enter the traffic pattern via the crosswind leg.

Have numbers....—Used by pilots to inform air traffic control that they have received runway, wind, and altimeter information only.

high speed taxiway, exit, or **turnoff**—A long radius taxiway designed and provided with lighting or marking to define the path of aircraft traveling a high speed (up to 60 knots) from the runway center to a point on the center of the taxiway. Also referred to as long radius exit or turn-off taxiway. The high speed taxiway is designed to expedite aircraft turning off the runway after landing, which reduces runway occupancy time.

hold or **holding procedure**—A predetermined maneuver that keeps aircraft within a specified airspace while awaiting further clearance from air traffic control. Also used during ground operations to keep aircraft within a specified area or at a specified point while awaiting further clearance from air traffic control.

How do you hear me?—A question relating to the quality of the transmission or to determine how well the transmission is being received.

Ident....—A request from air traffic control for a pilot to activate the aircraft transponder identification feature. This will help the controller to confirm an aircraft identity or to identify an aircraft.

If feasible, reduce (or increase) speed to....—Pilots are expected to maintain a speed of plus or minus 10 knots from the specified speed. It is an air traffic control procedure used to request pilots to adjust aircraft speed to a specified value for the purpose of providing desired spacing. Naturally, if the request is not feasible the pilot must report that to the controller and probably explain why compliance is not feasible.

IFR conditions—Weather conditions below the minima for flight under visual flight rules.

instrument meteorological conditions—Meteorological conditions expressed in terms of visibility, distance from cloud, and ceiling less than the minima specified for visual meteorological conditions.

Immediately....—Used by air traffic control when such action compliance is required to avoid an imminent situation.

instrument flight rules (IFR)—Rules governing the procedures for conducting instrument flight. Also a term used by pilots and controllers to indicate type of flight plan.

intersecting runways—Two or more runways that cross or meet within their lengths.

intersection—A point defined by any combination of courses, radials, or bearings or two or more navigational aids; the term is also used to describe the point where two runways, a runway and a taxiway, or two taxiways cross or meet.

intersection departure or **intersection takeoff**—A takeoff proposed on a runway from an intersection.

I say again....—The message shall be repeated.

known traffic—With respect to air traffic control clearances, means aircraft whose altitude, position, and intentions are known by the controller(s).

landing or **takeoff area**—Any locality either on land, water, or structures, including airports, heliports, and intermediate landing fields, that is used, or intended to be used, for the landing and takeoff of aircraft, whether or not facilities are provided for the shelter or servicing of aircraft or accommodations available for receiving or discharging passengers or cargo.

landing direction indicator—A device that visually indicates the direction in which landings and takeoffs should be made.

landing roll—The distance from the point of touchdown to the point where the aircraft can be brought to a stop or exit the runway.

landing sequence—The order that aircraft are positioned in for landing.

local traffic—Aircraft operating in the traffic pattern or within sight of the tower, or aircraft known to be departing or arriving from flight in local practice areas, or aircraft executing practice instrument approaches at the airport.

low approach—An approach over an airport or runway following an instrument approach or visual flight rules approach including the go-around maneuver where the pilot intentionally does not make contact with the runway.

Maintain....—Remain at the specified altitude, or in other instances of air traffic control instruction, the term is used in its literal sense, for instance, "Maintain visual flight rules."

Make short approach....—Used by air traffic control to inform a pilot to alter his traffic pattern so as to make a short final approach.

Mayday, mayday, mayday....—The international radiotelephony distress signal that indicates imminent and grave danger and that immediate assistance is requested.

microburst—A small downburst with outbursts of damaging winds extending 2.5 miles or fewer. In spite of its small horizontal scale, an intense microburst could induce wind speeds as high as 150 knots.

minimum fuel—Indicates that an aircraft's fuel supply has reached a state where, upon reaching the destination, it can accept little or no delay. This is not an emergency situation but merely indicates an emergency situation is possible if any undue delay occurs.

Missed approach....—A term used by the pilot to inform a controller that he is executing a missed approach.

movement area—The runways, taxiways, and other areas of an airport that are utilized for taxiing, takeoff, and landing of aircraft, exclusive of loading ramps and parking areas. At airports with a tower, specific approval for entry onto the movement area must be obtained from ground controller.

Negative....—"No" or "permission not granted" or "that is not correct."

Negative contact....—Used by pilots to inform air traffic control that previously issued traffic (reported traffic) is not in sight, perhaps followed by the pilot's request for the controller to provide assistance in avoiding the traffic. Also used by pilots to inform a controller that they were unable to contact a different controller on different frequency.

night—The time between the end of evening civil twilight and the beginning of morning civil twilight, as published in the *American Air Almanac*, converted to local time. Note: Civil twilight ends in the evening when the center of the sun's disk is six degrees below the horizon and begins in the morning when the center of the sun's disk is six degrees below the horizon.

Numerous targets vicinity....—A traffic advisory issued by a controller to advise pilots that targets on the radarscope are too numerous to issue individually.

obstacle—An existing object, object of natural growth, or terrain at a fixed geographical location or that might be expected at a fixed location within a prescribed area with reference to which vertical clearance is or must be provided during flight operation.

obstruction—Any object or obstacle exceeding the obstruction standard specified by FAR Part 77, Subpart C.

offset parallel runways—Staggered runways having centerlines that are parallel.

option approach—An approach requested and conducted by a pilot that will result in either a touch-and-go, low approach, missed approach, stop and go, or full-stop landing.

Out....—The conversation is ended and no response is expected.

outer area (of an airport radar service area, ARSA)—Nonregulatory airspace surrounding designated ARSA airports wherein ATC provides radar vectoring and sequencing on a full-time basis for all participating VFR aircraft. The service provided in the outer area is called "ARSA service," which includes:

- IFR/IFR standard IFR separation.
- IFR/VFR traffic advisories and conflict resolution.
- VFR/VFR traffic advisories and, as appropriate, safety alerts.

The normal radius will be 20 nautical miles with certain variations based on site-specific requirements. The outer area extends outward from the primary ARSA airport and extends from the radio/radar coverage up to the ceiling of the approach control's delegated airspace excluding the ARSA and other relevant airspace.

Over....—Indicates the conclusion of a transmission; a response is expected.

Pan-Pan—The international radiotelephony urgency signal. Repeating it three times indicates uncertainty or alert followed by the nature of the urgency.

parallel runways—Two or more runways at the same airport, whose centerlines are parallel. In addition to runway number, parallel runways are designated as L for left, R for right, and if three runways exist, C for the center runway.

Pilot's discretion....—When used in conjunction with altitude assignments, means that ATC has offered the pilot the option of starting climb or descent whenever he wishes and conducting the climb or descent at any rate he wishes. He may temporarily level off at any altitude. However, once he has vacated an altitude, he may not return to that altitude.

progressive taxi—Precise taxi instructions given to a pilot unfamiliar with the airport or issued in stages as the aircraft proceeds along the taxi route.

radar advisory—The provision of advice and information based on radar observations.

radar approach control facility—A terminal ATC facility that uses radar and nonradar capabilities to provide approach control services to aircraft arriving, departing, or transiting airspace controlled by the facility.

radar arrival—An aircraft arriving at an airport served by a radar facility and in radar contact with the facility.

Radar contact....—Used by ATC to inform an aircraft that it is identified on the radar display and radar flight following will be provided until radar identification is terminated. Radar service might also be provided within the limits of necessity and capability. The term is also used to inform the controller that the aircraft is identified and approval is granted for the aircraft to enter the receiving controller's airspace.

Radar contact lost....—Used by ATC to inform a pilot that radar identification of his aircraft has been lost. The loss might be attributed to several things, including the aircraft's merging with weather echoes or ground clutter, the aircraft's flying below radar line of sight, the aircraft's entering an area of poor radar return, or failure of the aircraft transponder or ground radar equipment.

radar service—A term that encompasses one or more of the following services, based on the use of radar that can be provided by a controller to a pilot of a radar identified aircraft: radar monitoring, radar navigational guidance, radar separation.

Radar service terminated....—Used by ATC to inform a pilot that he will no longer be provided any of the services that could be received while in radar contact. Radar service is automatically terminated without the pilot being advised in the several cases that are fully described in the AIM.

radar traffic advisories—Advisories issued to alert pilots to known or observed radar traffic that might affect the intended route of flight of their aircraft.

Read back....—Repeat my message back to me.

Report....—Used to instruct pilots to advise ATC of special information, for instance, "Report passing Hamilton VOR."

reporting point—A geographical location in relation to which the position of an aircraft is reported.

Resume own navigation....—Used by ATC to advise a pilot to resume his own navigation responsibility. It is used after completion of a radar vector or when radar contact is lost while the aircraft is being radar vectored.

Roger....—I have received all of your last transmission. It should not be used to answer a question requiring a yes or no answer.

runway—A defined rectangular area on a land airport prepared for the landing and takeoff run of aircraft along its length. Runways are normally numbered in relation to their magnetic direction rounded off to the nearest 10 degrees. (Surface winds are reported as related to magnetic north to correspond with runway headings.)

runway gradient—The average slope, measured in percent, between two ends or points on a runway. Runway gradient is depicted on government aerodrome sketches when total runway gradient exceeds 0.3 percent.

Runway heading....—The magnetic direction indicated by the runway number. When cleared to "maintain runway heading," pilots are expected to fly the heading indicated by the runway number, not the actual magnetic heading of the runway.

runway in use, active runway, or **duty runway**—Any runway or runways currently being used for takeoff or landing. When multiple runways are used, they are all considered active runways.

Say again....—Used to request a repeat of the prior transmission. Usually specifies transmission or a portion thereof not understood or received.

Say altitude....—Used by ATC to ascertain an aircraft's specific altitude. When the aircraft is climbing or descending, the pilot should state the indicated altitude rounded off to the nearest 100 feet.

Say heading....—Used by ATC to request an aircraft heading. The pilot should state the actual heading of the aircraft.

see and avoid—A visual procedure wherein pilots of aircraft flying in visual meteorological conditions, regardless of type of flight plan, are charged with the responsibility to observe the presence of other aircraft and to maneuver their aircraft as required to avoid the other aircraft. The definition specifically mentions aircraft that are "flying"; naturally any pilot would realize the importance of see and avoid while preparing for takeoff and while taxiing the aircraft.

segmented circle—A system of visual indicators that provide traffic pattern information at airports without operating control towers.

separation—Spacing of aircraft to achieve their safe and orderly movement in flight and while landing and taking off.

separation minima—The minimum longitudinal, lateral, or vertical distances by which aircraft are spaced through the application of air traffic control procedures.

Speak slower....—Used in verbal communications as a request to reduce speech rate.

special VFR conditions—Weather conditions in a control zone that are less than basic VFR and in which certain aircraft are permitted to operate under visual flight rules.

special VFR operations—Aircraft operating in accordance with clearances within control zones in weather conditions less than the basic VFR weather minima. Such operations must be requested by the pilot and approved by ATC.

Squawk (mode, code, or **function)**....—A request for a pilot to activate specific modes, codes, or functions on the aircraft transponder.

Stand by....—Means the controller or pilot must pause for a few seconds, usually to attend to other duties of higher priority. Also means to wait, as in "stand by for clearance." If a delay is lengthy, the caller should reestablish contact.

Stop altitude, mode, or **code squawk**....—Used by ATC to inform the pilot of an aircraft to turn off the automatic altitude reporting feature of the transponder. It is issued when the verbally reported altitude varies 300 feet or more from the automatic altitude report. "Mode" or "code" is stated when the controller wants a pilot to turn off that specific function.

stop and go—When an aircraft will land, make a complete stop on the runway, and then commence a takeoff from that point.

stopway—An area beyond the takeoff runway designated by the airport authorities as able to support an airplane during an aborted takeoff.

straight-in VFR approach—Entry into the traffic pattern by interception of the extended runway centerline (final approach course) without executing any other portion of the traffic pattern.

straight-in landing—A landing made on a runway aligned within 30 degrees of the final approach course, following completion of an instrument approach.

sunset and **sunrise**—The mean solar times of sunset and sunrise as published in the Nautical Almanac, converted to local standard time for the locality concerned. Within Alaska, the end of evening civil twilight and the beginning of morning civil twilight, as defined for each locality.

taxi—The movement of any airplane under its own power on the surface of an airport. Also, it describes the surface movement of helicopters equipped with wheels.

Taxi into position and hold....—Used by ATC to inform a pilot to taxi onto the departure runway in takeoff position and hold. It is not authorization for takeoff. It is used when takeoff clearance cannot immediately be issued because of traffic or other reasons.

taxi patterns—Patterns established to illustrate the desired flow of ground traffic for the different runways or airport area available for use.

terminal area—A general term used to describe airspace in which approach control service or airport traffic control service is provided.

terminal area facility—A facility providing air traffic control service for arriving and departing IFR, VFR, special VFR, and on occasion, en route aircraft.

tetrahedron—A device normally located on uncontrolled airports and used as a landing direction indicator. The small end of a tetrahedron points in the direction of landing. At controlled airports, the tetrahedron, if installed, should be disregarded because tower instructions supersede the indicator.

That is correct....—The understanding you have is right.

threshold—The beginning of that portion of the runway usable for landing.

time group—Four digits representing the hour and minutes from the 24-hour clock. Time groups without time zone indicators are understood to be UTC (Coordinated Universal Time). The term *zulu* is used when procedures require a reference to UTC. A time zone designator is used to indicate local time. The end and beginning of the day are shown by 2400 and 0000, respectively.

touch-and-go or **touch-and-go landing**—An operation by an aircraft that lands on and departs a runway without stopping or exiting the runway.

touchdown—The point at which an aircraft first makes contact with the landing surface.

touchdown zone—The first 3,000 feet of the runway, beginning at the threshold.

touchdown zone elevation—The highest elevation in the first 3,000 feet of the runway, beginning at the threshold. (The elevation is noted regarding instrument approaches.)

tower or **airport traffic control tower**—A terminal facility that uses air-to-ground communications, visual signaling, and other devices to provide services to aircraft operating in the vicinity of an airport or on the movement area. Authorizes aircraft to land or take off at the airport controlled by the tower or to transit the airport traffic area regardless of flight plan or weather conditions. A tower might also provide approach control services, radar or nonradar.

track—The actual flight path of an aircraft over the surface of the earth.

traffic—A term used by a controller to transfer radar identification of an aircraft to another controller for the purpose of coordinating separation action. Also a term used by a controller to refer to one or more aircraft.

traffic advisories—Advisories issued to alert pilots to other known or observed air traffic that might be in such proximity to the position or intended route of flight of their aircraft to warrant their attention. The word "traffic" followed by additional information, if known, is used to provide such advisories. Traffic advisory service is provided to the extent possible depending on higher priority duties of the controller or other limitations. Traffic advisories do not relieve the pilot of his responsibility to see and avoid other aircraft. Pilots are cautioned (by the definition) that there are many times when the controller is not able to give traffic advisories concerning all traffic in the aircraft's proximity. The FAA clarifies that when a pilot requests or is receiving traffic advisories, he should not assume that all traffic will be issued.

Traffic in sight....—Used by pilots to inform a controller that previously issued traffic is in sight.

Traffic no longer a factor....—Indicates that the traffic described in a previously issued traffic advisory is no longer a factor.

Unable....—Indicates inability to comply with a specific instruction, request, or clearance.

uncontrolled airspace—Uncontrolled airspace is that portion of the airspace that has not been designated as continental control area, control area, control zone, terminal control area, or transition area within which ATC has neither the authority nor the responsibility for exercising control over air traffic.

unicom—A nongovernment communication facility that provides airport information at certain airports. Locations and frequencies of unicoms are shown on aeronautical charts and in aeronautical publications.

upwind leg—A flight path parallel to the landing runway in the direction of landing.

urgency—A condition of being concerned about safety and of requiring timely but not immediate assistance.

vector—A heading issued to the pilot of an aircraft to provide navigational guidance by radar.

Verify....—Request confirmation of information.

vertical separation—Separation established by assignment of different altitudes or flight levels.

VFR aircraft or **flight**—An aircraft conducting flight in accordance with visual flight rules.

VFR conditions....—Weather conditions equal to or better than the minimum for flight under visual flight rules. When the term is used as part of an ATC clearance or authorization, all pilots that receive the authorization must comply with the visibility and distance from cloud criteria in FAR Part 91. Use of the term does not relieve the controllers of their responsibility to separate aircraft in certain controlled airspace as required in an ATC controller handbook.

visibility—The ability, as determined by atmospheric conditions and expressed in units of distance, to see and identify prominent unlighted objects by day and prominent lighted objects by night. Visibility is reported as statute miles, hundreds of feet, or meters.

visual flight rules (VFR)—Rules that govern the procedures for conducting flight under visual conditions. The term is also used in the United States to indicate weather conditions that are equal to or greater than minimum requirements. In addition, it is used by pilots and controllers to indicate type of flight plan.

visual meteorological conditions—Meterological conditions expressed in terms of visibility, distance from cloud, and ceiling equal to or better than specified minima.

visual separation—A means employed by ATC to separate aircraft in terminal areas.

vortices or **wing tip vortices**—Circular patterns of air created by the movement of an airfoil through the air when generating lift. As an airfoil moves through the atmosphere in sustained flight, an area of low pressure is created above it. The air flowing from the high pressure area to the low pressure area around and about the tips of the airfoil tends to roll up into two rapidly rotating vortices, cylindrical in shape. These vortices are the most characteristic features of aircraft wake turbulence, and their rotational force is dependent upon the wing loading, gross weight, and speed of the generating aircraft. The vortices from medium to heavy aircraft can be of extremely high velocity and hazardous to smaller aircraft.

wake turbulence—Phenomena resulting from the passage of an aircraft through the atmosphere. The term includes vortices, thrust stream turbulence, jet blast, jet wash, propeller wash, and rotor wash both on the ground and in the air.

When able....—When used with instructions, gives the pilot the latitude to delay compliance until a condition or event has been reconciled. Unlike "pilot discretion," when instructions are prefaced "when able," the pilot is expected to seek the first opportunity to comply. When a maneuver has been initiated, the pilot is expected to continue until the specifications of the instructions have been met. "When able" should not be used when expeditious compliance is required.

Wilco....—The message has been received, understood, and shall be complied with.

wind shear—A change in wind speed and/or direction in a short distance, resulting in a tearing or shearing effect. It can exist on a horizontal or vertical plane and occasionally on both simultaneously.

Words twice....—As a request, "Communication is difficult. Please say every phrase twice." As information, "Because communications are difficult, every phrase in this message will be spoken twice."

Appendix D
Private Pilot Airplane Single-Engine Land Practical Test Standards

THE MATERIAL CONTAINED IN THIS APPENDIX HAS BEEN EXTRACTED from the FAA publication, "Private Pilot Practical Test Standards for Airplane (Single-engine Land), FAA-S-8081-1A." These standards represent a new and higher level of competency which is being required for the private pilot certificate.

Use of the Private Pilot Practical Test Standards

This Private Pilot Practical Test Standards book has been published by the Federal Aviation Administration (FAA) to establish the standards for the private pilot certification practical tests for all aircraft categories and classes. FAA inspectors and designated pilot examiners will conduct practical tests in compliance with these standards. Flight instructors and applicants will find these standards helpful in practical test preparation.

Practical Test Standard Concept

FARs (Federal Aviation Regulations) specify the areas in which knowledge and skill must be demonstrated by the applicant before the issuance of a pilot certificate or rating. The FARs provide the flexibility to permit the FAA to publish practical test standards containing specific TASKS (procedures and maneuvers) in which pilot competency must be demonstrated. The FAA will add, delete, or revise TASKS whenever it is determined that changes are needed in the interest of safety. Adherence to provisions of the regulations and the practical test standards is mandatory for the evaluation of pilot applicants.

Flight Instructor Responsibility

An appropriately rated flight instructor is responsible for training the student to the acceptable standards as outlined in the objective of each TASK within the appropriate practical test standard. The flight instructor must certify that the applicant is able to perform safely as a private pilot and is competent to pass the required practical test for the certificate or rating sought.

Examiner* Responsibility

The examiner who conducts the practical test is responsible for determining that the applicant meets standards outlined in the objective of each TASK within the appropriate practical test standard. The examiner shall meet this responsibility by accomplishing an ACTION that is appropriate for each TASK. For each TASK that involves "knowledge only" elements, the examiner will orally quiz the applicant on those elements. For each TASK that involves both "knowledge and skill" elements, the examiner will orally quiz the applicant regarding knowledge elements and ask the applicant to perform the skill elements. The examiner will determine that the applicant's knowledge and skill meets the objective in all required TASKS. Oral questioning may be used at any time during the practical test.

Practical Test Standard Description

The AREAS OF OPERATION are phases of flight arranged in a logical sequence within each standard. They begin with the preparation of the flight and end with the conclusion of the flight. The examiner, however, may conduct the practical test in any sequence that results in a complete and efficient test.

The TASKS are procedures and maneuvers appropriate to an AREA OF OPERATION. The AIRCRAFT CATEGORIES AND CLASSES appropriate to the TASKS are abbreviated in capital letters within parentheses immediately following each TASK. The meaning of each abbreviation follows:

    ASEL   Airplane Single-Engine Land
    AMEL   Airplane Multiengine Land

---

*The word "examiner" is used to denote either the FAA inspector or FAA designated pilot examiner who conducts an official flight test.

ASES	Airplane Single-Engine Sea
AMES	Airplane Multiengine Sea
RH	Rotorcraft Helicopter
RG	Rotocraft Gyroplane
G	Glider (including powered glider)
LA	Lighter-Than-Air Airship
LB	Lighter-Than-Air Free Balloon

The number after the pilot operation relates that TASK to the regulatory requirement.

The REFERENCE identifies the publication(s) that describe(s) the TASK. Descriptions of TASKS are not included in the standards because this information can be found in the listed references. Publications other than those listed may be used for references if their content conveys substantially the same meaning as the referenced publications.

References upon which this practical test book is based include:

FAR Part 61	Certification: Pilots and Flight Instructors
FAR Part 91	General Operating and Flight Rules
AC 00-6	Aviation Weather
AC 00-45	Aviation Weather Services
AC 61-13	Basic Helicopter Handbook
AC 61-21	Flight Training Handbook
AC 61-23	Pilot's Handbook of Aeronautical Knowledge
AC 61-27	Instrument Flying Handbook
AC 61-84	Role of Preflight Preparation
AC 67-2	Medical Handbook for Pilots
AC 91-13	Cold Weather Operation of Aircraft
AC 91-55	Reduction of Electrical Systems Failure following Engine Starting
AIM	Airman's Information Manual

NOTE: The latest revision of the references cited should be used.

The OBJECTIVE lists, in sequence, the important elements that must be satisfactorily performed to demonstrate competency in a TASK. The OBJECTIVE includes:

- Specifically what the applicant should be able to do.
- The conditions under which the TASK is to be performed.
- The minimum acceptable standards of performance.

151

Use of the Practical Test Book

The FAA requires that each practical test be conducted in strict compliance with the appropriate practical test standards for the issuance of a pilot certificate or rating. When using the practical test book, the examiner must evaluate the applicant's knowledge and skill in sufficient depth to determine that the standards of performance listed for all TASKS are met.

When the examiner determines, during the performance of one TASK, that the knowledge and skill objective of another TASK is met, it may not be necessary to require the performance of the other TASK.

The examiner may, for any valid reason, elect to evaluate certain TASKS orally, such TASKS include those that do not conform to the manufacturer's recommendations or operating limitations or those that are impracticable, such as night flying, operations over congested areas, or unsuitable terrain, etc.

The examiner is not required to follow the precise order in which the AREAS OF OPERATION and TASKS appear in each section. The examiner may change the sequence or combine TASKS with similar objectives to conserve time. Examiners will develop a plan of action that includes the order and combination of tasks to be demonstrated by the applicant in a manner that will result in an efficient and valid test. The examiner shall accurately evaluate the applicant's ability to perform safely as a pilot throughout the practical test.

Suggested examples of combining TASKS are:

- Descending turns may be combined with high altitude emergencies.
- Rectangular course may be combined with airport traffic pattern.
- Navigation during flight by reference to instruments may be combined with visual navigation.

Other TASKS with similar OBJECTIVES may be combined to conserve time. However, the OBJECTIVES of all TASKS must be demonstrated and evaluated at some time during the practical test.

Examiners will place special emphasis upon areas of aircraft operation which are most critical to flight safety. Among these areas are correct aircraft control and sound judgment in decision making. Although these areas may not be shown under each TASK, they are essential to flight safety and will receive careful evaluation throughout the practical test. If these areas are shown in the OBJECTIVE, additional emphasis will be placed on them. The examiner will also emphasize stall/spin awareness, spatial disorientation, collision avoidance, wake turbulence avoidance, low-level wind shear, use of the checklist, and other areas as directed by future revisions of this standard.

Use of Distractions During Practical Tests

Numerous studies indicate that many accidents have occurred when the pilot's attention has been distracted during various phases of flight. Many accidents have resulted from engine failure during takeoffs and landings where safe flight was possible if the pilot had used correct control technique and divided attention properly.

Distractions that have been found to cause problems are:

- Preoccupation with situations inside or outside the cockpit.
- Maneuvering to avoid other traffic.
- Maneuvering to clear obstacles during takeoffs, climbs, approaches, or landings.

To strengthen this area of pilot training and evaluation, the examiner will provide realistic distractions throughout the practical test. Many distractions may be used to evaluate the applicant's ability to divide attention while maintaining safe flight. Some examples of distractions are:

- Simulating engine failure;
- Simulating radio tuning and communications;
- Identifying a field suitable for emergency landings;
- Identifying features or objects on the ground;
- Reading the outside air temperature gauge;
- Removing objects from the glove compartment or map case;
- Questioning by the examiner.

Aircraft and Equipment Requirements

The applicant is required to provide an appropriate and airworthy aircraft for the practical test. The aircraft must be equipped for, and its operating limitations must not prohibit the pilot operations required on the test.

Satisfactory Performance

The ability of an applicant to perform the required TASKS is based on:

- Executing TASKS within the aircraft's performance capabilities and limitations, including use of the aircraft's systems.
- Executing emergency procedures and maneuvers appropriate to the aircraft.
- Piloting the aircraft with smoothness and accuracy.
- Exercising good judgment.
- Applying aeronautical knowledge.

• Showing mastery of the aircraft within the standards outlined in this book, with the successful outcome of a TASK never seriously in doubt.

Unsatisfactory Performance

If, in the judgment of the examiner, the applicant does not meet the standards of performance of any TASK performed, the associated PILOT OPERATION is failed and therefore, the practical test is failed.

The examiner or applicant may discontinue the test at any time after the failure of a PILOT OPERATION makes the applicant ineligible for the certificate or rating sought. The test will be continued ONLY with the consent of the applicant. If the test is discontinued, the applicant is entitled to credit for only those TASKS satisfactorily performed. However, during the retest and at the discretion of the examiner, any TASK may be re-evaluated, including those previously passed.

The tolerances stated in the OBJECTIVE represent the minimum performance expected in good flying conditions.

Consistently exceeding tolerances or failure to take prompt corrective action when tolerances are exceeded, is unsatisfactory performance.

Any action, or lack thereof, by the applicant which requires corrective intervention by the examiner to maintain safe flight will be disqualifying. The applicant shall use proper and effective scanning techniques to clear the area before performing maneuvers. Ineffective performance in these areas will be disqualifying.

I. PREFLIGHT PREPARATION

Task: Certificates and Documents (ASEL)

PILOT OPERATION - 1

References: FAR Parts 61 and 91; AC 61-21, AC 61-23; Pilot's Handbook and Flight Manual.

Objective. To determine that the applicant:

1. Exhibits knowledge by explaining the appropriate—
   a. Pilot certificate, privileges and limitations
   b. Medical certificate, class and duration.
   c. Personal pilot logbook or flight record.
   d. FCC station license and operator's permit, as required.
2. Exhibits knowledge by locating and explaining the significance and importance of the—
   a. Airworthiness and registration certificates.
   b. Operating limitations, handbooks, or manuals.
   c. Equipment list.

d. Weight and balance data.

e. Maintenance requirements and appropriate records.

Task: Obtaining Weather Information (ASEL)

NOTE: This TASK is NOT required for the addition of a single-engine land class rating.

PILOT OPERATION - 1

References: AC 00-6, AC 00-45, AC 61-21, AC 61-23, AC 61-84.

Objective. To determine that the applicant:

1. Exhibits knowledge of aviation weather information by obtaining, reading, and analyzing -
   a. Weather reports and forecasts.
   b. Weather charts.
   c. Pilot weather reports.
   d. SIGMETs and AIRMETs.
   e. Notices to Airmen.
   f. Wind-shear reports.
2. Makes a competent go/no-go decision based on the available weather information.

Task: Determining Performance and Limitations (ASEL)

PILOT OPERATION - 1

References: AC 61-21, AC 61-23, AC 61-84; Airplane Handbook and Flight Manual.

Objective. To determine that the applicant:

1. Exhibits knowledge by explaining airplane weight and balance, performance, and limitations, including adverse aerodynamic effects of exceeding the limits.
2. Uses available and appropriate performance charts, tables, and data.
3. Computes weight and balance, and determines that weight and center of gravity will be within limits during all phases of the fight.
4. Calculates airplane performance, considering density altitude, wind, terrain, and the other pertinent conditions.
5. Describes the effects of atmospheric conditions on airplane performance.
6. Makes a competent decision on whether the required performance is within the operating limitations of the airplane.

Task: Cross-Country Flight Planning (ASEL)

NOTE: This TASK is NOT required for the addition of a single-engine land class rating.

PILOT OPERATION - 7

References: AC 61-21, AC 61-23, AC 61-84.

Objective. To determine that the applicant:

1. Exhibits knowledge by planning, within 30 minutes, a VFR cross-country flight of a duration near the range of the airplane, considering fuel and loading.
2. Selects and uses current and appropriate aeronautical charts.
3. Plots a course for the intended route of flight with fuel stops, if necessary.
4. Selects prominent en route check points.
5. Computes the flight time, headings, and fuel requirements.
6. Selects appropriate radio navigation aids and communication facilities.
7. Identifies airspace, obstructions, and alternate airports.
8. Extracts pertinent information from the Airport/Facility Directory and other flight publications, including NOTAMs.
9. Completes a navigation log.
10. Completes and files a VFR flight plan.

Task: Airplane Systems (ASEL)

PILOT OPERATION - 1

References: AC 61-21; Airplane Handbook and Flight Manual.

Objective. To determine that the applicant exhibits knowledge by explaining the airplane systems and operation including, as appropriate:

1. Primary flight controls and trim.
2. Wing flaps, leading edge devices, and spoilers.
3. Flight instruments.
4. Landing gear.
5. Engine.
6. Propeller.
7. Fuel system.
8. Hydraulic system.
9. Electrical system.
10. Environmental system.
11. Oil system.
12. Deice and anti-ice systems.

13. Avionics.
14. Vacuum system.

Task: Aeromedical Factors (ASEL)

PILOT OPERATION - 1
References: AC 61-21, AC 67-2; AIM.

Objective. To determine that the applicant:

1. Exhibits knowledge of the elements related to aeromedical factors, including the symptoms, effects, and corrective action of -
   a. Hypoxia.
   b. Hyperventilation.
   c. Middle ear and sinus problems.
   d. Spatial disorientation.
   e. Motion sickness.
   f. Carbon monoxide poisoning.
2. Exhibits knowledge of the effects of alcohol and drugs, and the relationship to flight safety.
3. Exhibits knowledge of nitrogen excesses during scuba dives, and how this affects a pilot or passenger during flight.

II. GROUND OPERATIONS

Task: Visual Inspection (ASEL)

PILOT OPERATION - 1
References: AC 61-21; Airplane Handbook and Flight Manual.

Objective. To determine that the applicant:

1. Exhibits knowledge of airplane visual inspection by explaining the reasons for checking all items.
2. Inspects the airplane by following a checklist.
3. Determines that the airplane is in condition for safe flight emphasizing-
   a. fuel quantity, grade, and type.
   b. fuel contamination safeguards.
   c. fuel venting.
   d. oil quantity, grade, and type.
   e. fuel, oil, and hydraulic leaks.
   f. flight controls.
   g. structural damage.
   h. exhaust system.
   i. tiedown, control lock, and wheel chock removal.

j. ice and frost removal.

k. security of baggage, cargo, and, equipment.

Task: Cockpit Management (ASEL)

PILOT OPERATION - 1
Reference: AC 61-21.

Objective. To determine that the applicant:

1. Exhibits knowledge of cockpit management by explaining related safety and efficiency factors.
2. Organizes and arranges the material and equipment in an efficient manner.
3. Ensures that the safety belts and shoulder harnesses are fastened.
4. Adjusts and locks the rudder pedals and pilot's seat to a safe position and ensures full control movement.
5. Briefs occupants on the use of safety belts and emergency procedures.
6. Exhibits adequate crew coordination.

Task: Starting Engine (ASEL)

PILOT OPERATION - 1
References: AC 61-21, AC 61-23, AC 91-13, AC 91-55; Airplane Handbook and Flight Manual.

Objective. To determine that the applicant:

1. Exhibits knowledge by explaining engine starting procedures, including starting under various atmospheric conditions.
2. Performs all the items on the checklist.
3. Accomplishes correct starting procedures with emphasis on -
   a. positioning the airplane to avoid creating hazards.
   b. determining that the area is clear.
   c. adjusting the engine controls.
   d. setting the brakes.
   e. preventing airplane movement after engine start.
   f. avoiding excessive engine RPM and temperatures.
   g. checking the engine instruments after engine start.

Task: Taxiing (ASEL)

PILOT OPERATION - 2
Reference: AC 61-21.

Objective. To determine that the applicant:

1. Exhibits knowledge by explaining safe taxi procedures.
2. Adheres to signals and clearances, and follows the proper taxi route.
3. Performs a brake check immediately after the airplane begins moving.
4. Controls taxi speed without excessive use of brakes.
5. Recognizes and avoids hazards.
6. Positions the controls for the existing wind conditions.
7. Avoids careless and reckless operations.

Task: Pretakeoff Check (ASEL)

PILOT OPERATION - 1
References: AC 61-21; Airplane Handbook and Flight Manual

Objective. To determine that the applicant:

1. Exhibits knowledge of the pre-takeoff check by explaining the reasons for checking all items.
2. Positions the airplane to avoid creating hazards.
3. Divides attention inside and outside of the cockpit.
4. Accomplishes the checklist items.
5. Ensures that the airplane is in safe operating condition.
6. Reviews the critical takeoff performance airspeeds and distances.
7. Describes takeoff emergency procedures.
8. Obtains and interprets takeoff and departure clearances.

Task: Postflight Procedures (ASEL)

PILOT OPERATION - 3
References: AC 61-21; Airplane Handbook and Flight Manual.

Objective. To determine that the applicant:

1. Exhibits knowledge by explaining the postflight procedures, including taxiing, parking, shutdown, securing, and postflight inspection.
2. Selects and taxies to the designated or suitable parking area, considering wind conditions and obstructions.
3. Parks the airplane properly.
4. Follows the recommended procedure for engine shutdown, cockpit securing, and deplaning passengers.
5. Secures the airplane properly.
6. Performs a satisfactory postflight inspection.

III. AIRPORT AND TRAFFIC PATTERN OPERATIONS

NOTE: This AREA OF OPERATION is NOT required for the addition of a single-engine land class rating.

Task: Radio Communications and ATC Light Signals (ASEL)

PILOT OPERATION - 2
References: AC 61-21, AC 61-23; AIM.

Objective. To determine that the applicant:

1. Exhibits knowledge by explaining radio communication, ATC light signals, procedures at controlled and uncontrolled airports, and prescribed procedures for radio failure.
2. Selects the appropriate frequencies for the facilities to be used.
3. Transmits requests and reports using the recommended standard phraseology.
4. Receives, acknowledges, and complies with radio communications.

Task: Traffic Pattern Operations (ASEL)

PILOT OPERATION - 2
References: AC 61-21, AC 61-23; AIM.

Objective. To determine that the applicant:

1. Exhibits knowledge by explaining traffic pattern procedures at controlled and uncontrolled airports, including collision, wind shear, and wake turbulence avoidance.
2. Follows the established traffic pattern procedures according to instructions or rules.
3. Corrects for wind drift to follow the appropriate ground track.
4. Maintains proper spacing from other traffic.
5. Maintains the traffic pattern altitude, ± 100 feet.
6. Maintains the desired airspeed, ± 10 knots.
7. Completes the prelanding cockpit checklist.
8. Maintains orientation with the runway in use.

Task: Airport and Runway Marking and Lighting (ASEL)

PILOT OPERATION - 2
References: AC 61-21; AIM.

Objective. To determine that the applicant:

1. Exhibits knowledge by explaining airport and runway markings and lighting aids.
2. Identifies and interprets airport, runway, taxiway marking, and lighting aids.

IV. TAKEOFFS AND CLIMBS

Task: Normal and Crosswind Takeoffs and Climbs (ASEL)

PILOT OPERATION - 5
References: AC 61-21; Airplane Handbook and Flight Manual.

Objective. To determine that the applicant:

1. Exhibits knowledge by explaining the elements of normal and crosswind takeoffs and climbs, including airspeeds, configurations, and emergency procedures.
2. Selects the recommended wing-flap setting.
3. Aligns the airplane on the runway centerline.
4. Applies aileron deflection properly.
5. Advances the throttle smoothly to maximum allowable power.
6. Checks engine instruments.
7. Maintains directional control on runway centerline.
8. Adjusts aileron deflection during acceleration.
9. Rotates at the recommended[1] airspeed and accelerates to V_Y and establishes wind-drift correction.
10. Establishes the pitch attitude for V_Y and maintains V_Y $\pm$ 5 knots.
11. Retracts the wing flaps, as recommended, or at a safe altitude.
12. Retracts the landing gear, if retractable, after a positive rate of climb has been established and a safe landing can no longer be accomplished on the remaining runway.
13. Maintains takeoff power to a safe maneuvering altitude.
14. Maintains a straight track over the extended runway centerline until a turn is required.
15. Completes after-takeoff checklist.

NOTE: If a crosswind condition does not exist, the applicant's knowledge of the TASK will be evaluated through oral testing.

---

[1]The term "recommended" refers to the manufacturer's recommendation. If the manufacturer's recommendation is not available, the description in AC 61-21 will be used.

Task: Short-Field Takeoff and Climb (ASEL)

PILOT OPERATION - 8

References: AC 61-21; Airplane Handbook and Flight Manual.

Objective. To determine that the applicant:

1. Exhibits knowledge by explaining the elements of a short-field takeoff and climb, including the significance of appropriate airspeeds and configurations, emergency procedures, and expected performance for existing operating conditions.
2. Selects the recommended wing-flap setting.
3. Positions the airplane at the beginning of the takeoff runway aligned on the runway centerline.
4. Advances the throttle smoothly to maximum allowable power.
5. Maintains directional control on the runway centerline.
6. Rotates at the recommended airspeed and accelerates to V_X.
7. Climbs at V_X or recommended airspeed, $+5$, -0 knots until obstacle is cleared, or until at least 50 feet above the surface, then accelerates to V_Y and maintains V_Y, ± 5 knots.
8. Retracts the wing flaps, as recommended, or at a safe altitude.
9. Retracts the landing gear, if retractable, after a positive rate of climb has been established and a safe landing can no longer be accomplished on the remaining runway.
10. Maintains takeoff power to a safe maneuvering altitude.
11. Maintains a straight track over the extended runway centerline until a turn is required.
12. Completes after-takeoff checklist.

Task: Soft-Field Takeoff and Climb (ASEL)

PILOT OPERATION - 8

References: AC 61-21; Airplane Handbook and Flight Manual.

Objective. To determine that the applicant:

1. Exhibits knowledge by explaining the elements of a soft-field takeoff and climb, including the significance of appropriate airspeeds and configurations, emergency procedures, and hazards associated with climbing at an airspeed less than V_X.
2. Selects the recommended wing-flap setting.
3. Taxies onto the takeoff surface at a speed consistent with safety.
4. Aligns the airplane on takeoff path, without stopping, and advances the throttle smoothly to maximum allowable power,

5. Adjusts and maintains pitch attitude which transfers the weight from the wheels to the wings as rapidly as possible.
6. Maintains directional control on the center of the takeoff path.
7. Lifts off at the lowest possible airspeed and remains in ground effect while accelerating.
8. Accelerates to and maintains V_X + 5, − 0 knots, if obstructions must be cleared, otherwise to V_Y ± 5 knots.
9. Retracts the wing flaps, as recommended, and at a safe altitude.
10. Retracts the landing gear, if retractable, after a positive rate of climb has been established and a landing can no longer be accomplished on the remaining runway.
11. Maintains takeoff power to a safe maneuvering altitude.
12. Maintains a straight track over the center of the extended takeoff path until a turn is required.
13. Completes after-takeoff checklist.

V. CROSS-COUNTRY FLYING

NOTE: This AREA OF OPERATION is NOT required for the addition of a single-engine land class rating.

Task: Pilotage and Dead Reckoning (ASEL)

PILOT OPERATION - 7
References: AC 61-21, AC 61-23.

Objective. To determine that the applicant:
1. Exhibits knowledge by explaining pilotage and dead reckoning techniques and procedures.
2. Follows the preplanned course solely by visual reference to landmarks.
3. Identifies landmarks by relating the surface features to chart symbols.
4. Navigates by means of precomputed headings, groundspeed, and elapsed time.
5. Combines pilotage and dead reckoning.
6. Verifies the airplane position within 3 nautical miles of the flight planned route at all times.
7. Arrives at the en route checkpoints and destination ± 5 minutes of the initial or revised ETA.
8. Corrects for, and records, the differences between preflight fuel, groundspeed, and heading calculations and those determined en route.
9. Maintains the selected altitudes, within ± 200 feet.

10. Maintains the desired heading, $\pm 10°$.

11. Follows the climb, cruise, and descent checklists.

Task: Radio Navigation (ASEL)

PILOT OPERATION - 7
References: AC 61-21, AC 61-23.

Objective. To determine that the applicant:

1. Exhibits knowledge by explaining radio navigation, equipment, procedures, and limitations.
2. Selects and identifies the desired radio facility.
3. Locates position relative to the radio navigation facility.
4. Intercepts and tracks a given radial or bearing.
5. Locates position using cross radials or bearings.
6. Recognizes or describes the indication of station passage.
7. Recognizes signal loss and takes appropriate action.
8. Maintains the appropriate altitude, ± 200 feet.

Task: Diversion (ASEL)

PILOT OPERATION - 7
References: AC 61-21, AC 61-23.

Objective. To determine that the applicant:

1. Exhibits knowledge by explaining the procedures for diverting, including the recognition of adverse weather conditions.
2. Selects an appropriate alternate airport and route.
3. Diverts toward the alternate airport promptly.
4. Makes a reasonable estimate of heading, groundspeed, arrival time, and fuel consumption to the alternate airport.
5. Maintains the appropriate altitude, ± 200 feet.

Task: Lost Procedures (ASEL)

PILOT OPERATION - 7
References: AC 61-21, AC 61-23.

Objective. To determine that the applicant:

1. Exhibits knowledge by explaining lost procedures, including the reasons for -
   a. Maintaining the original or an appropriate heading, identifying landmarks, and climbing, if necessary.

b. Proceeding to and identifying the nearest concentration of prominent landmarks.

c. Using available radio navigation aids or contacting an appropriate facility for assistance.

d. Planning a precautionary landing if deteriorating visibility and/or fuel exhaustion is imminent.

2. Selects the best course of action when given a lost situation.

VI. FLIGHT BY REFERENCE TO INSTRUMENTS

NOTE: This AREA OF OPERATION is NOT required for the addition of a single-engine land class rating.

Task: Straight-and-Level Flight (ASEL)

PILOT OPERATION - 6
References: AC 61-21, AC 61-23, AC 61-27.

Objective. To determine that the applicant:

1. Exhibits knowledge by explaining flight solely by reference to instruments as related to straight-and-level flight.
2. Makes smooth and coordinated control applications.
3. Maintains straight-and-level flight for at least 3 minutes.
4. Maintains the desired heading, ± 10°.
5. Maintains the desired altitude, ± 100 feet.
6. Maintains the desired airspeed, ± 10 knots.

Task: Straight, Constant Airspeed Climbs (ASEL)

PILOT OPERATION - 6
References: AC 61-21, AC 61-23, AC 61-27.

Objective. To determine that the applicant:

1. Exhibits knowledge by explaining flight solely by reference to instruments as related to straight, constant airspeed climbs.
2. Establishes the climb pitch attitude and power setting on an assigned heading.
3. Makes smooth and coordinated control applications.
4. Maintains the desired heading, ± 10°.
5. Maintains the desired airspeed, ± 10 knots.
6. Levels off at the desired altitude, ± 100 feet.

Task: Straight, Constant Airspeed Descents (ASEL)

PILOT OPERATION - 6
References: AC 61-21, AC 61-23, AC 61-27.

Objective. To determine that the applicant:

1. Exhibits knowledge by explaining flight solely by reference to instruments as related to straight, constant airspeed descents.
2. Determines the minimum safe altitude at which the descent should be terminated.
3. Establishes the descent configuration, pitch, and power setting on the assigned heading.
4. Makes smooth and coordinated control applications.
5. Maintains the desired heading, ± 10°.
6. Maintains the desired airspeed, ± 10 knots.
7. Levels off at the desired altitude, ± 100 feet.

Task: Turns to Headings (ASEL)

PILOT OPERATION - 6
References: AC 61-21, AC 61-23, AC 61-27.

Objective. To determine that the applicant:

1. Exhibits knowledge by explaining flight solely by reference to instruments as related to turns to headings.
2. Enters and maintains approximately a standard-rate turn with smooth and coordinated control applications.
3. Maintains the desired altitude, ± 100 feet.
4. Maintains the desired airspeed, ± 10 knots.
5. Maintains the desired bank angle.
6. Rolls out at the desired heading, ± 10°.

Task: Unusual Flight Attitudes (ASEL)

PILOT OPERATION - 6
References: AC 61-21, AC 61-23, AC 61-27.
NOTE: Unusual flight attitudes, such as a start of a power-on spiral or an approach to a climbing stall, shall not exceed 45° bank or 10° pitch from level flight.

Objective. To determine that the applicant:

1. Exhibits knowledge by explaining flight solely by reference to instruments as related to unusual flight attitudes.

2. Recognizes unusual flight attitudes promptly.
3. Properly interprets the instruments.
4. Recovers to a stabilized level flight attitude by prompt, smooth, coordinated control, applied in the proper sequence.
5. Avoids excessive load factor, airspeed, and stall.

Task: **Radio Aids and Radar Services (ASEL)**

PILOT OPERATION - 6
References: AC 61-21, AC 61-23, AC 61-27.

Objective. To determine that the applicant:

1. Exhibits knowledge by explaining radio aids and radar services available for use during flight solely by reference to instruments.
2. Selects, tunes, and identifies the appropriate facility.
3. Follows verbal instructions or radio navigation aids for guidance.
4. Determines the minimum safe altitude.
5. Maintains the desired altitude, ± 100 feet.
6. Maintains the desired heading, ± 10°.

VII. FLIGHT AT CRITICALLY SLOW AIRSPEEDS

Task: **Full Stalls—Power Off (ASEL)**

PILOT OPERATION - 4
Reference: AC 61-21.

Objective. To determine that the applicant:

1. Exhibits knowledge by explaining the aerodynamic factors and flight situations that may result in full stalls—power on, including proper recovery procedures, and hazards of stalling during uncoordinated flight.
2. Selects an entry altitude that will allow the recoveries to be completed no lower than 1,500 feet AGL.
3. Establishes the normal approach or landing configuration and airspeed with the throttle closed or at a reduced power setting.
4. Establishes a straight glide or a gliding turn with a bank angle of 30°, ± 10°, in coordinated flight.
5. Establishes and maintains a landing pitch attitude that will induce a full stall.
6. Recognizes the indications of a full stall and promptly recovers by decreasing the angle of attack, leveling the wings, and adjusting the

power, as necessary, to regain normal flight attitude.

7. Retracts the wing flaps and landing gear (if retractable) and establishes straight-and-level flight or climb.

8. Avoids secondary stalls, excessive airspeed, excessive altitude loss, spins, and flight below 1,500 feet AGL.

Task: Full Stalls—Power On (ASEL)

PILOT OPERATION - 4
Reference: AC 61-21.

Objective. To determine that the applicant:

1. Exhibits knowledge by explaining the aerodynamic factors and flight situations that may result in full stalls—power on, including proper recovery procedures, and hazards of stalling during uncoordinated flight.

2. Selects an entry altitude that will allow the recoveries to be completed no lower than 1,500 feet AGL.

3. Establishes takeoff or normal climb configuration.

4. Establishes takeoff or climb airspeed before applying takeoff or climb power. (Reduced power may be used to avoid excessive pitch-up during entry only.)

5. Establishes and maintains a pitch attitude straight ahead or in a turn with a bank angle of 20°, ± 10°, that will induce a full stall.

6. Applies proper control to maintain coordinated flight.

7. Recognizes the indications of a full stall and promptly recovers by decreasing the angle of attack, leveling the wings, and adjusting the power, as necessary, to regain normal flight attitude.

8. Retracts the wing flaps and landing gear (if retractable) and establishes straight-and-level flight or climb.

9. Avoids secondary stall, excessive airspeed, excessive altitude loss, spin, and flight below 1,500 feet AGL.

Task: Imminent Stalls—Power On and Power Off (ASEL)

PILOT OPERATION - 4
Reference: AC 61-21.

Objective. To determine that the applicant:

1. Exhibits knowledge by explaining the aerodynamic factors associated with imminent stalls (power on and power off), an awareness of speed loss in different configurations, and the procedure for resuming normal flight attitude.

2. Selects an entry altitude that will allow recoveries to be completed no lower than 1,500 feet AGL.
3. Establishes either a takeoff, a climb, or an approach configuration with the appropriate power setting.
4. Establishes a pitch attitude on a constant heading, ± 10°, or 20° bank turns, ± 10°, that will induce an imminent stall.
5. Applies proper control to maintain coordinated flight.
6. Recognizes and recovers from imminent stalls at the first indication of buffeting or decay of control effectiveness by reducing angle of attack and adjusting power, as necessary, to regain normal flight attitude.
7. Avoids full stall, secondary stall, excessive airspeed, excessive altitude change, spin, and flight below 1,500 feet AGL.

Task: Maneuvering at Critically Slow Airspeed (ASEL)

PILOT OPERATION - 4
Reference: AC 61-21.

Objective. To determine that the applicant:

1. Exhibits knowledge by explaining the flight characteristics and controllability associated with maneuvering at critically slow airspeeds.
2. Selects and entry altitude that will allow the maneuver to be performed no lower than 1,500 feet AGL.
3. Establishes and maintains a critically slow airspeed while -
   a. In coordinated straight and turning flight in various configurations and bank angles, and
   b. In coordinated departure climbs and landing approach descents in various configurations.
4. Maintains the desired altitude, ± 100 feet, when a constant altitude is specified, and levels off from climbs and descents, ± 100 feet.
5. Maintains the desired heading during straight flight, ± 10°.
6. Maintains the specified bank angle, ± 10°, in coordinated flight.
7. Maintains a critically slow airspeed, + 5, − 0 knots.

Task: Constant Altitude Turns (ASEL)

PILOT OPERATION - 10
Reference: AC 61-21.

Objective. To determine that the applicant:

1. Exhibits knowledge by explaining the performance factors associated with constant altitude turns, including increased load factors, power required, and overbanking tendency.

2. Selects an altitude that will allow the maneuver to be performed no lower than 1,500 feet AGL.

3. Establishes an airspeed which does not exceed the airplane design maneuvering airspeed.

4. Enters a 360° turn maintaining a bank angle of 40° to 50° in coordinated flight.

5. Divides attention between airplane control and orientation.

6. Rolls out at the desired heading, ± 10°.

7. Maintains the desired altitude, ± 100 feet.

VIII. FLIGHT MANEUVERING BY REFERENCE TO GROUND OBJECTS

NOTE: This AREA OF OPERATION is NOT required for the addition of a single-engine land class rating.

Task: Rectangular Course (ASEL)

PILOT OPERATION - 3
Reference: AC 61-21.

Objective. To determine that the applicant:

1. Exhibits knowledge by explaining wind-drift correction in straight-and-turning flight, and the relationship of the rectangular course to airport traffic patterns.

2. Selects a suitable reference area.

3. Enters a left or right pattern at a desired distance from the selected reference area and at 600 to 1,000 feet AGL.

4. Divides attention between airplane control and ground track, and maintains coordinated flight.

5. Applies the necessary wind-drift corrections during straight-and-turning flight to maintain the desired ground track.

6. Maintains the desired altitude, ± 100 feet.

7. Maintains the desired airspeed, ± 10 knots.

8. Avoids bank angles in excess of 45°.

9. Reverses course, as directed by the examiner.

Task: S-Turns Across a Road (ASEL)

PILOT OPERATION - 3
Reference: AC 61-21.

Objective. To determine that the applicant:

1. Exhibits knowledge by explaining the procedures and wind-drift correction associated with S-turns.
2. Selects a suitable ground reference line.
3. Enters perpendicular to the selected reference line at 600 to 1,000 feet AGL.
4. Divides attention between airplane control and ground track, and maintains coordinated flight.
5. Applies the necessary wind-drift correction to track a constant radius turn on each side of the selected reference line.
6. Reverses the direction of turn directly over the selected reference line.
7. Maintains the desired altitude, ± 100 feet.
8. Maintains the desired airspeed, ± 10 knots.

Task: Turns Around a Point (ASEL)

PILOT OPERATION - 3
Reference: AC 61-21.

Objective. To determine that the applicant:

1. Exhibits knowledge by explaining the procedures and wind-drift correction associated with turns around a point.
2. Selects suitable ground reference points.
3. Enters a left or right turn at a desired distance from the selected reference point at 600 to 1,000 feet AGL.
4. Divides attention between airplane control and ground track, and maintains coordinated flight.
5. Applies the necessary wind-drift corrections to track a constant-radius turn around the selected reference point.
6. Maintains the desire altitude, ± 100 feet.
7. Maintains the desired airspeed, ± 10 knots.

IX. NIGHT FLIGHT OPERATIONS

NOTE: This AREA OF OPERATION is NOT required for the addition of a single-engine land class rating. However, if the applicant is to be evaluated on night flying operations, then the examiner must evaluate elements 1 through 3. Elements 4 through 8 may be evaluated at the option of the examiner.

Night flight operations will be evaluated ONLY if the applicant meets night flying regulatory requirements. If this AREA OF OPERATION is not evaluated, the applicant's certificate will bear the limitation, "Night Flying Prohibited."

Task: Night Flight (ASEL)

PILOT OPERATION - 9
References: AC 61-21, AC 67-2.

Objective. To determine that the applicant:

1. Explains preparation, equipment, and factors essential to night flight.
2. Determines airplane, airport, and navigation lighting.
3. Exhibits knowledge by explaining night flying procedures, including safety precautions and emergency actions.
4. Inspects the airplane by following the checklist which includes items essential for night flight operations.
5. Starts, taxies, and performs pretakeoff check adhering to good operating practices.
6. Performs takeoffs and climbs with emphasis on visual references.
7. Navigates and maintains orientation under VFR conditions.
8. Approaches and lands adhering to good operating practices for night flight operations.

X. EMERGENCY OPERATIONS

Task: Emergency Approach and Landing (Simulated) (ASEL)

PILOT OPERATION - 10
References: AC 61-21; Airplane Handbook and Flight Manual.

Objective. To determine that the applicant:

1. Exhibits knowledge by explaining approach and landing procedures to be used in various emergencies.
2. Establishes and maintains the recommended best-glide airspeed and configuration during simulated emergencies.
3. Selects a suitable landing area within gliding distance.
4. Plans and follows a flight pattern to the selected landing area, considering altitude, wind, terrain, obstructions, and other factors.
5. Follows an appropriate emergency checklist.
6. Attempts to determine the reason for the simulated malfunction.
7. Maintains positive control of the airplane.
   NOTE: Examiner should terminate the emergency approach at or above minimum safe altitude.

Task: System and Equipment Malfunctions (ASEL)

PILOT OPERATION - 10
References: AC 61-21; Airplane Handbook and Flight Manual.

Objective. To determine that the applicant:

1. Exhibits knowledge by explaining causes of, indications of, and pilot actions for, malfunctions of various systems and equipment.
2. Analyzes the situation and takes appropriate action for simulated emergencies such as—

    a. Partial power loss.
    b. Rough running engine or overheat.
    c. Carburetor or induction icing.
    d. Loss of oil pressure.
    e. Fuel starvation.
    f. Engine compartment fire.
    g. Electrical system malfunction.
    h. Gear or flap malfunction.
    i. Door opening in flight.
    j. Trim inoperative.
    k. Loss of pressurization.
    l. Other malfunctions.

XI. APPROACHES AND LANDINGS

Task: Normal and Crosswind Approaches and Landings (ASEL)

PILOT OPERATION - 5
References: AC 61-21; Airplane Handbook and Flight Manual.

Objective. To determine that the applicant:

1. Exhibits knowledge by explaining the elements of normal and crosswind approaches and landings, including airspeeds, configurations, crosswind limitations, and related safety factors.
2. Maintains the proper ground track on final approach.
3. Establishes the approach and landing configuration and power required.
4. Maintains the recommended approach airspeed, ± 5 knots.
5. Makes smooth, timely, and correct control application during the final approach and transition from approach to landing roundout.

6. Touches down smoothly at approximate stalling speed, at or within 500 feet beyond a specified point, with no appreciable drift, and the airplane longitudinal axis aligned with the runway centerline.
7. Maintains directional control, increasing aileron deflection into the wind, as necessary, during the after-landing roll.
NOTE: If a crosswind condition does not exist, the applicant's knowledge of the TASK will be evaluated through oral testing.

Task: Forward Slips to Landing (ASEL)

PILOT OPERATION - 5
Reference: AC 61-21.

Objective. To determine that the applicant:

1. Exhibits knowledge by explaining the elements of a forward slip to a landing, including the purpose, technique, limitation, and the effect on airspeed indications.
2. Establishes a forward slip at a point from which a landing can be made in a desired area using the recommended airspeed and configuration.
3. Maintains a ground track aligned with the runway centerline.
4. Maintains an airspeed which results in minimum floating during the landing roundout.
5. Recovers smoothly from the slip.
6. Touches down smoothly at approximate stalling speed, at and within 500 feet beyond a specified point, with no appreciable drift, and the airplane longitudinal axis aligned with the runway centerline.
7. Maintains directional control during the after-landing roll.

Task: Go-Around (ASEL)

PILOT OPERATION - 5
References: AC 61-21; Airplane Handbook and Flight Manual.

Objective. To determine that the applicant:

1. Exhibits knowledge by explaining the elements of the go-around procedure, including proper decision, recommended airspeeds, drag effect of wing flaps and landing gear, and coping with undesirable pitch and yaw.
2. Makes a proper decision to go around.
3. Applies takeoff power and establishes the proper pitch attitude to attain the recommended airspeed.
4. Retracts the wing flaps, as recommended, and at a safe altitude.

5. Retracts the landing gear, if retractable, after a positive rate of climb has been established.
6. Trims the airplane and climbs at V_Y $\pm$ 5 knots, and tracks the appropriate traffic pattern.

Task: Short-Field Approach and Landing (ASEL)

PILOT OPERATION - 8
References: AC 61-21; Airplane Handbook and Flight Manual.

Objective. To determine that the applicant:

1. Exhibits knowledge by explaining the elements of a short-field approach and landing, including airspeed, configuration, and related safety factors.
2. Considers obstructions, landing surface, and wind conditions.
3. Selects a suitable touchdown point.
4. Establishes the short-field approach and landing configuration, airspeed, and descent angle.
5. Maintains control of the descent rate and the recommended airspeed, $\pm$ 5 knots, along the extended runway centerline.
6. Touches down at or within 200 feet beyond a specified point, with minimum float, no appreciable drift, and the airplane longitudinal axis aligned with the runway centerline.
7. Maintains directional control during the after-landing roll.
8. Applies braking and controls, as necessary, to stop in the shortest distance consistent with safety.

Task: Soft-Field Approach and Landing (ASEL)

PILOT OPERATION - 8
References: AC 61-21; Airplane Handbook and Flight Manual.

Objective. To determine that the applicant:

1. Exhibits knowledge by explaining the elements of a soft-field approach and landing procedure, including airspeeds, configurations, operations on various surfaces, and related safety factors.
2. Evaluates obstructions, landing surface, and wind conditions.
3. Establishes the recommended soft-field approach and landing configuration and airspeed.
4. Maintains recommended airspeed, $\pm$ 5 knots, along the extended runway centerline.
5. Touches down smoothly at minimum descent rate and groundspeed,

with no appreciable drift, and the airplane longitudinal axis aligned with runway centerline.

6. Maintains directional control during the after-landing roll.
7. Maintains proper position of flight controls and sufficient speed to taxi on soft surface.

APPLICANT'S PRACTICAL TEST CHECKLIST (SUGGESTED)

Acceptable Aircraft

☐ View-Limiting Device (if applicable)
☐ Aircraft Documents:
    Airworthiness Certificate
    Registration Certificate
    Operating Limitations
☐ Aircraft Maintenance Records:
    Airworthiness Inspections
☐ FCC Station License

Personal Equipment

☐ Current Aeronautical Charts
☐ Computer and Plotter
☐ Flight Plan Form
☐ Flight Logs
☐ Current AIM

Personal Records

☐ Pilot Certificate
☐ Medical Certificate
☐ Completed FAA Form 8710-1, Airman Certificate and/or
    Rating Application
☐ AC Form 8080-2, Airman Written Test Report
☐ Logbook with Instructor's Endorsement
☐ Notice of Disapproval (if applicable)
☐ Approved School Graduation Certificate (if applicable)
☐ FCC Radiotelephone Operator Permit (if applicable)
☐ Examiner's Fee (if applicable)

Appendix E
Takeoff and Landing Procedural Review

SAFE OPERATING PRACTICES HAVE THEIR ROOTS IN FUNDAMENTAL flying techniques that rely on acceptable limits commonly found in test standards prepared by the FAA. A recent set of standards developed by the FAA contains acceptable levels of performance to meet requirements for certification as a recreational pilot. The levels of performance might be less lenient for advanced certificates, but the intent of acceptably safe performance is a recognizable goal for a pilot trying to improve his ability and become a safer operator.

Reviewing selected parts of the recreational pilot flight test standards, and striving to meet the goals, should improve the margin of safety for any pilot, starting with the normal and crosswind takeoff:

- Elements of normal and crosswind takeoffs, including airspeeds, configurations, and emergency procedures.

- Verification of wind direction.

- Align aircraft on the runway centerline.

- Full aileron deflection in the direction of the crosswind.

- Advance the throttle smoothly to maximum allowable power.

- Check engine instruments.

- Maintain directional control down runway centerline.

- Adjust aileron deflection in crosswind conditions during acceleration.

- Rotate at the aircraft manufacturer's recommended airspeed, accelerate to best rate-of-climb airspeed, and in crosswind conditions establish wind-drift correction.

- Establish the pitch angle for the best rate-of-climb airspeed and maintain that airspeed plus or minus 10 knots.

- Retract wing flaps as recommended or at a safe altitude.

- Maintain takeoff power to a safe maneuvering altitude.

- Maintain a straight track over the extended runway centerline until a turn is required.

- Complete after-takeoff checklist.

A potentially lifesaving maneuver that should be mastered by all pilots is the *go-around* to initiate another landing attempt. The recreational pilot test standards offer an effective review of the go-around:

- Understand the elements of the go-around procedure, including timely decision-making, recommended airspeeds, drag effect of the wing flaps, and undesirable pitch and yaw tendencies.

- Make a timely decision to go around from a rejected landing.

- Apply takeoff power and establish the proper pitch attitude to attain the aircraft manufacturer's recommended airspeed.

- Retract the wing flaps as required and recommended by the aircraft manufacturer, or retract at a safe altitude.

- Trim the aircraft and climb at the best rate-of-climb airspeed and track the appropriate airport traffic pattern.

Finally, the recreational pilot test standards offer an effective review of normal and crosswind landings:

- Understand elements of normal and crosswind landings, including crosswind limitations, airspeeds, configurations, and related safety factors.

- Maintain the proper ground track on final approach.

- Establish the required approach and landing configuration with proper power.

- Maintain the recommended approach speed within plus or minus 5 knots.

- Make smooth, timely, and correct control applications during the final approach, and transition from the approach to landing roundout.

- Touch down smoothly at approximate stalling speed, beyond and within 500 feet of a specified point, with no appreciable drift, and with the airplane longitudinal axis aligned with the runway centerline.

- Maintain directional control, increasing aileron deflection into the wind, as necessary, during the after-landing roll.

Appendix F
Accident Reviews

REVIEWING TAKEOFF AND LANDING ACCIDENTS IS ONE WAY TO avoid catastrophic results of unwanted situations: learning the lesson before suffering the consequences. Accident reports that are filed by FAA and NTSB investigators become fertile soil for plowing up the pitfalls of takeoffs and landings.

Accident reports reveal only the facts of the investigation: pilot and passenger narratives; ground witness narratives; ATC narratives in the form of audio tapes and radar video tapes; the results of examination of the wreckage for faulty components or obvious malfunctions; weather; pilot qualifications; and more.

Conclusions at the end of every investigation are not carved in granite. Based upon those facts, the best investigation can only report "probable cause," according to every report. A probable cause might seem quite obvious, but you never know what else might have caused an accident.

The following sampling of takeoff and landing accidents states pertinent facts, the probable cause, and other related factors, as determined by the investigation. For the sake of anonymity, date, location, and specific aircraft make and model information are not revealed, and accident reports used for this review do not include pilot name or certificate number.

Beyond stating the facts, these reviews include noninvestigative supposition and conjecture that is purely intended to stimulate reader application of the facts to his aircraft operating consciousness. The suppositions and conjecture are indirectly related to the NTSB's published accident report, but they are not intended to relate to respective individuals, manufacturers, or components.

WEATHER WISDOM

The pilot reported to ATC that the airport was in sight; ATC cleared the aircraft for a visual approach. There was no further radio contact with the pilot. Witnesses who saw the aircraft on a left downwind said that it flew into a thundershower. Wreckage was found in a bay 1.25 miles north of the runway. The aircraft apparently struck the water with the left wing low. The aircraft, flight controls, and engine were apparently functioning normally at the time of the accident.

A level 3 thunderstorm was at the crash site at the time of the accident, according to radar photographs. Ceiling was reported at 2,000 feet, broken, with rain and fog in visual meteorological conditions, daylight hours. The instrument-rated pilot had received a full weather briefing from a commercial weather vendor and had filed in IFR flight plan. Flight into known adverse weather probably caused the accident, according to the NTSB. The pilot and sole passenger died.

When all occupants of an aircraft die in an accident, analysis is difficult without their insight. Had they lived, they might have explained that the clouds had seemed harmless and that they had continued to fly without untoward concern; the lesson might be to never underestimate the hidden power of a cloud, especially a cloud that is producing precipitation, regardless of how many times you might have flown through a similar cloud in the past. In this case, the pilot probably should have requested more information from ATC regarding the intensity of the storm. Ideally the pilot would have practiced see-and-avoid, simply deviating from a standard approach path around the thundershower, within regulatory, operational and personal safety margins, while maintaining visual contact with the airport, preferably the active runway.

The pilot might have been distracted by cockpit duties. Imagine referring to an approach plate or other aeronautical chart to obtain frequencies or other pertinent airport data with your head down for approximately one minute. Upon raising your head, visual references, which would be necessary for the approach, have vanished because the aircraft is in instrument meteorological conditions. A moment of hesitation while hoping to regain a visual reference means that during an approach to landing, the aircraft has probably descended more than it would descend if an immediate climb had been established by referencing cockpit instruments. Critical height above ground level could dwindle rapidly and by the time remedial action were initiated, the aircraft would probably descend farther, before the positive climb was underway.

In this case, avoidance was the apparent key to survival, noted by the NTSB. The conjecture would imply developing a personal plan to initiate a climb whenever instrument conditions are encountered and operational parameters, plus safety concerns, allow such a maneuver. Take command of the situation and change the situation in your favor by creating a safety margin, rather than hoping that the situation will change on its own and provide the safety margin on a silver platter. Perhaps one consideration is a belief that if a bad situation has arisen, expect it to worsen unless you take action to stifle unsafe developments and most likely overcome the effects.

WHO HAS THE AIRCRAFT?

A flight instructor was demonstrating an emergency landing to a private pilot. The two pilots became confused about who was supposed to be flying the aircraft, which resulted in a commitment to land. The aircraft sustained substantial damage when it veered off a gravel road during the roll-out. The accident was probably caused by improper in-flight planning/decision making on the part of the instructor, inadequate crew coordination during the simulated emergency procedure, plus, again on the part of the certified flight instructor, during the landing roll, not maintaining directional control that caused an inadvertent ground loop. The pilots were not injured.

Probably the most important instruction every flight instructor should give is establishing a crystal clear understanding of who is controlling the aircraft. Whenever possible, the instructor and student should establish eye contact, speak distinctly, and return the comment, "You have the aircraft," with an equally clear response of, "I have the aircraft," when aircraft control is established. Granted, during an unusual attitude, eye contact might be impossible; that is when a stern and distinct voice exchange should be practiced. Whenever there is the slightest doubt on the part of either of two pilots in the cockpit of a dual-control aircraft regarding who is controlling that aircraft, they must clarify the matter. Ask and ensure who has responsibility for control.

TAKE NOTICE

The pilot of a high-performance single-engine aircraft received a PATWAS telephone weather briefing prior to a cross-country flight. Nearly 250 hours were in the pilot's logbook at the time of the accident, more than half the time in the same make and model, averaging 20 hours a month for the past three months. Weather at the time of the accident was a factor: daylight, wind 210 degrees at 5 knots, visibility 10 statute miles, and scattered clouds at 2,000 feet.

According to the NTSB report, at the end of the cross-country flight, during the landing roll, the aircraft began to slide to the left. The pilot was unable to regain control due to patchy snow and ice on the runway. The aircraft left the runway and hit a snow bank. No mechanical factors were reported. A NOTAM was in effect at the time of the accident that reported the runway was closed due to icy conditions. Runway status, according to the report, was ice covered.

Not maintaining directional control and poor preflight planning/preparation probably caused the accident, according to the NTSB. Factors related to the accident included a crosswind condition, icy terrain, and not identifying NOTAMs. Four persons, the pilot and three passengers, were not injured; the aircraft was substantially damaged.

Safety of pilot, passengers, and persons on the ground is taken into account when an airport is temporarily closed. Someone or a group of people studies a situation and determines that safe operation of an aircraft is unlikely due to a particular set of circumstances. In this case, the runway was probably a sheet of ice, and that means traction was nil.

Knowledge of an icy runway and the accurate airport status is as close as a telephone consultation. If a pilot requests applicable NOTAMs directly from a briefer via telephone, from DUAT via computer terminal, or en route from an appropriate facility via two-way radio communications, that runway closure will be reported and appropriate action can be taken: postpone the flight or select an alternate destination.

TOUCHY TAILWHEEL

The tailwheel aircraft swerved to the left during one takeoff attempt, which was subsequently aborted. The aircraft again swerved to the left during a second takeoff attempt, ran off the runway, and nosed over in loose sand. The pilot reportedly had made 10 takeoffs and landings in the same aircraft, believing that in this instance the tailwheel had become stuck in an off-center position. An airworthiness inspector found no evidence during a post-accident inspection that would explain the reported loss of directional control. The commercial/multi-engine pilot had seven hours in the make and model; 1,250 total time; 1,100 multi-engine. Wind was calm with no relevant weather conditions. The NTSB stated that lack of experience was a factor in the accident that left the pilot and one other person uninjured. The board said in its report that the pilot did not maintain directional control, which caused an inadvertent ground loop and probably caused the accident.

When any shortcoming is suspected in an aircraft, do not operate the aircraft. That broad statement would keep hundreds, perhaps thousands, of pilots grounded for many years to come. However, reasonable application of the concept might prevent accidents like this one. The pilot had made only 10 takeoffs and landings in this aircraft, when on the 11th takeoff the aircraft swerved so suddenly that the takeoff was aborted. A moment or two for a mental checklist of what-ifs, plus a subsequent careful execution of the recommended checklist for that aircraft, might have prompted a revelation that the tailwheel was not operating properly. Beyond that, a cautious high speed taxi test might have revealed deteriorating controllability that might have stopped upon aborting the taxi test. If the problem could not be isolated by checklists and operational tests, then perhaps a second attempt at takeoff would have been possible.

TAMPERING TROUBLE

The pilot and three passengers were not injured when the aircraft crashed during an emergency landing that was executed immediately after takeoff due to developing engine problems. Prior to the flight, an internal failure of the engine's vacuum pump prompted the pilot of the aircraft to remove the pump from the engine; the pilot did not install a cover plate on the vacuum pump's accessory mounting hole. After takeoff on the local flight, the pilot noticed the oil pressure was dropping and the engine temperature was rising. An attempt to return to the airport failed, and the pilot was forced to land in a cotton field after the engine seized. The absence of a vacuum pump, the total loss of engine oil, the seized engine, and the improper maintenance and modification by the pilot probably caused the accident, according to the NTSB.

Never alter a powerplant or an airframe and fly that airplane without consulting FAR Part 43 for allowable preventive maintenance performed by the pilot. Most pre-takeoff checklists note proper operation of the vacuum system within allowable limits indicated on the vacuum gauge on the instrument panel; use the checklist prior to every start-up and takeoff. The checklist might seem mundane and boring, but the printed routine can help a pilot relax because he does not have to think about what comes next, regardless of the repetition and familiarity, instead concentrating on verification of each checklist item. That routine of incremental go-no-go decisions fosters safe flying habits.

TERRIBLE TERRAIN

No injuries were reported when the tailwheel aircraft crashed during takeoff from an off-airport rural area. The commercial pilot with 1,000 hours, 250 in make and model, attempted to take off from a rough and soft strip. The aircraft nosed over when its main landing gear hit an exceptionally soft spot in the surface of the runway during the takeoff roll, causing substantial damage. Visual meteorological conditions prevailed, with 25-knot winds reported. The pilot later claimed that the accident could have been prevented if the landing site had been more carefully selected and the extremely soft ground avoided. The board concurred and determined that the accident was probably caused by unsuitable terrain selected by the pilot. The soft terrain was cited as a factor in the accident.

Pilots become complacent when every takeoff is on a hard surface runway. Unless a NOTAM or other advisory is received, the pilot can expect the runway of a public-use airport to be safe. That picture changes rapidly when the aircraft is operated from an unimproved runway, accurately described as a strip. Alaska bush pilots have a tried-and-true method of operating from a safe strip: physical examination. When landing, the simplist procedure is to make a low pass over the strip—ideally flying on the right side of the runway boundary with the centerline seen outside the left window—and examine the surface for tall grass, depressions, cracked earth, holes, standing water, mud, animals, obstructions, and the like. Consider applying climb trim to the controls, creating pressure for a firm but not overpowering resistance to maintain level flight during the low pass; any distraction that causes the pilot to relax the forward pressure means that the aircraft gradually climbs, rather than gradually descending. Prior to takeoff from an unimproved strip, walk over the runway or drive over the runway in a car or truck. If the vehicle cannot make a safe pass along one route, for instance the very center, try another straightline pathway on the runway, perhaps along each side, if width permits. The absence of a straightline pathway means the takeoff should be at the very least postponed.

ENGINE FAILURE

Shortly after sunrise, the aircraft took off on a cross-country flight with the pilot and one passenger on board. The private pilot had nearly 200 hours total time, most logged in the make and model; biennial and currency were up-to-date. Visual meteorological conditions prevailed upon takeoff, with a 12-knot wind, 10 statute miles visibility, scattered clouds at 5,000 feet, and an overcast layer at 25,000 feet. During the initial climbout, as the aircraft climbed through approximately 200 feet above ground level, the powerplant completely failed. A forced landing in a plowed field substantially damaged the aircraft and seriously injured the pilot and passenger. Investigators subsequently examined the engine and found that the number 1 piston had broken up, then was nearly pulverized by internal impacts. Remaining pistons were intact; however, a dye penetrant inspection revealed a fracture development in the casting line in the number 2 piston that was identical to the fracture location of the number 1 piston. Total failure of the piston (engine assembly) probably caused the accident, the board said, and the rough and uneven character of the plowed field was a contributing factor.

A suitable emergency landing site might have been difficult to locate in this instance, or the primary landing site could not have been reached. Constant awareness of terrain features might be difficult to develop, but recall for a moment the difficulties that you originally endured to establish adequate control of an aircraft for solo privileges: the effort paid off and the constant awareness of control faded into second nature.

Perhaps awareness of terrain features from the moment of takeoff until landing can become second nature and subsequently pay off some day. Simply focus on the ground occasionally during a typical scan for conflicting air traffic. (Focusing on different areas increases the possibility of focusing on any conflicting traffic.) Study the surface for the aircraft's proximity to any area that might be safe haven in case of an emergency. Study a sectional chart and locate airports that might suffice.

If an aircraft fuel system requires switching from one tank to another, make the switch close to an en route airport; if the engine fails and a restart is unsuccessful, that airport is close at hand. Descent to a routine landing narrows possible emergency landing sites; however, terrain features and obstructions are more apparent and less likely to cause last minute problems during an emergency landing.

Index

Other Bestsellers of Related Interest

THE ART OF INSTRUMENT FLYING
—2nd Edition—J. R. Williams
". . . as complete and up-to-date as an instrument book can be." —*Aero Magazine*

Williams has updated his comprehensive guide to include flight director, Loran-C, and Omega navigational systems; en route, area, TCA, and SID/STAR reference charts reflect current designations. The book addresses all elements of IFR flight. The first edition won the 1989 Best Technical Book award of the Western Region of the Aviation/Space Writers Association. 352 pages, 113 illustrations. Book No. 3654, $19.95 paperback, $31.95 hardcover

AIRCRAFT SYSTEMS: Understanding Your Airplane—David A. Lombardo

Designed to enhance your understanding of general aviation flying safety, this book thoroughly explains each separate operating system of your aircraft in an easy-to-follow style. A compilation of articles that originally ran as a continuing series in *Private Pilot* magazine, this book's 31 chapters are organized into four sections: power plant, electrical systems, aircraft systems, and instrumentation. Each system is covered from the pilot's point of view. 272 pages, 111 illustrations. Book No. 2423, $18.95 paperback only

IMPROVE YOUR FLYING SKILLS:
Tips from a Pro—Donald J. Clausing

Learn firsthand the professional attitudes, flying standards, and everyday procedures practiced by airline and corporate aircraft captains. Leading off with an overview of the basics of flying VFR and IFR, the author gives in-depth coverage of all the things that make up advanced, no-nonsense airmanship. Among the topics covered: flight planning, cruise control, types of approaches, weather flying, filing IFR, radio procedures, and "BILAHS" (Briefing, IFR, Log, Alternate, Hazardous weather). 224 pages, 42 illustrations. Book No. 3328, $14.95 paperback, $24.95 hardcover

PASSING THE FAA WRITTEN EXAM SERIES:
Commercial; Instrument; Private Pilot
—each by Tom McQueen

This series is the easiest, most cost-effective way to help you earn your wings—or seek higher ratings. Each volume is like a course in itself. The first section of each chapter presents all the possible questions along with only their correct answer. And the second section of each chapter boosts your comprehension by providing a detailed explanation for each question. The following categories for each certificate classification are covered: Federal Aviation Regulations, Aerodynamics, Performance, Weight and Balance, Airplane Instruments, Systems and Engines, Airports, Airspace and Air Traffic Control, Navigation, Flight Physiology, Weather Theory and Reports, Instrument Procedures, Fundamentals of Instruction, and Multi-engine (in *Commercial* only). Each guide provides you with the questions that can appear on the written exam, along with the correct answers. All material has been compiled directly from the most up-to-date government sources. Whether you're a prospective commercial, instrument, or private pilot, or a private pilot seeking the higher instrument rating or commercial certificate, these excellent, low-cost guides will help you pass the FAA written exams with flying colors.

Passing the FAA Written Exam: Private Pilot
144 pages, 49 illustrations. Book No. 3581, $9.95 paperback only

Passing the FAA Written Exam: Instrument
240 pages, 162 illustrations. Book No. 3580, $11.95 paperback only

Passing the FAA Written Exam: Commercial
128 pages, illustrated. Book No. 3579, $9.95 paperback only

AIM/FAR 1991—TAB/AERO Staff

Fully revised for 1991, this source provides complete information on federal regulations affecting general aviation. You'll find all the flight information, procedures, and rules you need to make flight plans, go/no-go decisions, study for FAA written exams and flight tests, and in countless other situations. Every effort has been made to make this the most current, accurate and comprehensive pilot resource available. Don't fly without it. 576 pages, illustrated. Book No. 24391, $11.95 paperback only

THE PILOT'S GUIDE TO WEATHER REPORTS, FORECASTS & FLIGHT PLANNING
—Terry T. Lankford

This comprehensive guide to aviation weather for all pilots offers clear explanations, real-life examples, and effective illustrations. It shows you how to access weather services efficiently, translate briefings correctly, and apply reports and forecasts to specific preflight and inflight situations to expand your margin of safety. 397 pages, 123 illustrations. Book No. 3582, $19.95 paperback, $29.95 hardcover

Prices Subject to Change Without Notice.

Look for These and Other TAB Books at Your Local Bookstore

To Order Call Toll Free 1-800-822-8158
(in PA, AK, and Canada call 717-794-2191)

or write to TAB Books, Blue Ridge Summit, PA 17294-0840.

Title	Product No.	Quantity	Price

☐ Check or money order made payable to TAB Books

Charge my ☐ VISA ☐ MasterCard ☐ American Express

Acct. No. _____ Exp. _____

Signature: _____

Name: _____

Address: _____

City: _____

State: _____ Zip: _____

Subtotal $ _____

Postage and Handling
($3.00 in U.S., $5.00 outside U.S.) $ _____

Add applicable state and local
sales tax $ _____

TOTAL $ _____

TAB Books catalog free with purchase; otherwise send $1.00 in check or money order and receive $1.00 credit on your next purchase.

Orders outside U.S. must pay with international money order in U.S. dollar.

TAB Guarantee: If for any reason you are not satisfied with the book(you order, simply return it (them) within 15 days and receive a fu refund. B